RULE OF LAW,
MISRULE OF MEN

RULE OF LAW, MISRULE OF MEN

Elaine Scarry

A Boston Review Book

THE MIT PRESS Cambridge, Mass. London, England

MIT Press books may be purchased at special quantity
discounts for business or sales promotional use. For
information, please email special_sales@mitpress.mit.edu or
write to Special Sales Department, The MIT Press,
55 Hayward Street, Cambridge, MA 02142.

This book was set in Adobe Garamond by *Boston Review*
and was printed and bound in the United States of America.

Library of Congress Cataloging-in-Publication Data
Scarry, Elaine.
  Rule of law, misrule of men / Elaine Scarry.
     p. cm.
  "A Boston Review Book."
  Includes bibliographical references.
  ISBN 978-0-262-01427-4 (hardcover : alk. paper) 1. Civil
rights—United States. 2. Rule of law—United States. 3. War
on Terrorism, 2001– —Political aspects—United States. 4.
United States—Armed Forces—Regulations. 5. War crime
trials—United States. I. Title.
  JC599.U5S345 2010
  973.931—dc22

                                        2009053482

10 9 8 7 6 5 4 3 2 1

For my brother and sister, Joe Scarry and Patricia Scarry Jones

CONTENTS

Introduction
(January 2010)

In January 2009, the Government Account-ability Office (GAO) delivered to Congress a report entitled "Homeland Defense: Actions Needed to Improve Air Sovereignty Alert Operations to Protect U.S. Airspace." The Air Sovereignty Alert program had been designed shortly after 9/11 to protect the U.S. population from air threats originating inside the country. It had arranged for eighteen air bases to be on "steady-state" ground alert with fighter jets ready to lift off at any moment. The Air Force had been given primary responsibility for enacting the program, which was presided over by the commander of NORAD.

But the GAO inquiry—which reviewed Air Sovereignty Alert Operations through September 2008—

found that many parts of the program had never been put into effect. The Air Force had abstained from carrying out the 140 directives it had been assigned at the program's outset, directives jointly formulated by NORAD, the Department of Defense, and the Air Force. Not only had the Air Force neglected to evaluate the readiness of airmen and equipment, it had not even "formally assigned Air Sovereignty Alert as a mission to the units and included it on the units' mission lists."[1] The report also found that NORAD had carried out almost no "risk assessment" studies of the eighteen sites.

Responding to inquiries from the GAO, the Air Force explained that it had neglected the program because it had given priority to its overseas obligations. NORAD attributed its own neglect to the fact that no explicit requirement for evaluating steady-state capabilities had been placed on it by the Department of Defense.

Salus populi—the well-being of the people—has since antiquity been understood as the central justification for having a government and for having a military. On September 11, 2001, the most expensive military in the world (unpracticed in defending the homeland) failed to protect the American people or even its own headquarters. Immediately following 9/11 and repeatedly in the seven years that followed, the Department of Defense identified the safety of the population as its primary aspiration.[2] But the 2009 Air Sovereignty Alert Report suggests that foreign wars were still its major concern.[3]

Between 2001 and 2008 (the years of the Bush-Cheney presidency), the safety of the people appears seldom to have been the central mission of the U.S. government. The indifference to air sovereignty (following a devastating attack from the air) is just one cinematic clip from a film that played before the population's eyes for eight years, as day after day the country watched coastal waters rise around a stranded population and saw young soldiers sent from home without body armor or vehicle armor and return in coffins that were not allowed to be photographed.[4]

But the book that follows is *not* about all those protective actions that the government failed to carry out, actions that would have been lawful and noble responses to the revelations of 9/11. It is instead about all the actions the government *did* carry out, relentless and ruthless acts of lawbreaking, actions designed to extend executive power, actions decoupled from (and steady degradations of) the aspiration encoded in salus populi.

Equally central to the book is a second subject, the sovereignty of the people, who, even under a government of misrule, retain the power to validate the rule of law: the population can refuse to participate in illegal acts even when instructed by government officials to do so (the subject of Chapter 1); the population can also work to ensure the prosecution of government leaders, if their illegal acts reach the level of perfidy, treachery, and war crime as defined by Constitutional law, international law, and our own Air Force, Army, and Navy handbooks (the subject of Chapters 2 and 3).

The chapters of this book were written at specific times throughout the eight-year Bush-Cheney period, and have been left almost unchanged:[5] written in *medias res*, they record presidential wrongs and forms of popular redress as they emerged into view. Chapter 1 focuses on the deformation of national law; Chapter 2, international law; Chapter 3, both national and international.

Is "deformation" too strong a word? The villages, towns, and cities across the United States that went on record saying they would not uphold the Patriot Act describe the locations within the Constitution they perceived to be at risk: among them, the First Amendment, the Fourth Amendment, the Fifth Amendment, the Eighth Amendment. Any one of these would be a cause for alarm. But as Chapter 1 shows, at risk was not just any one location within the Constitution but a central principle that radiates throughout its structure: the requirement that a government be transparent to its people, the people opaque to their governors. (For example, the ballot a citizen casts for a senatorial candidate is secret unless the citizen herself chooses to reveal her vote; she also chooses the persons to whom any such revelation is made; in contrast, every vote a senator casts in Congress must be open and on record, legible to the entire population.) The Bush administration sought to turn this structural principle inside out: through various forms of surveillance, the population would be unknowingly exposed to its governors, whose own actions would remain hidden from view.

Again in the international realm, large structures—even the foundation of law itself—were violated. The prohibition of torture is, as Chapters 2 and 3 argue, not one important law among many important laws. Rather, it is the philosophic foundation on which all other laws are created and without which our confidence in all other laws wavers. Three other acts that the international laws of war and our own military handbooks designate grave crimes are examined in Chapter 2: misusing the white flag and red cross; flying a false flag; and assassination, posting wanted-dead-or-alive signs, and issuing announcements of rewards.

Exactly how does an extra-legal universe get created? Some of the many fictions that went into creating this alternate world are chronicled in the pages that follow. But several key building blocks can be briefly surveyed here. First, a substantial head start on the building project is achieved if the architect already thinks of himself as an extra-legal agent: if a given law is X and the president announces "not-X," the law of X is cancelled just by virtue of that speech act. The President may announce that laws of long standing, such as the Geneva Conventions, are not in effect. He may take a law that has recently come into being though his own signature appended to Congressional legislation, and through a not-X signing statement eliminate the thing he a moment ago created. Especially helpful in this owning-while-disowning slide between X and not-X is any offshore geography leased but not owned (Guantánamo) or leased from a country that has itself leased it from a third country (Diego Garcia, leased by

Britain from Mauritania, and by the United States from Britain); supremely useful is a piece of ground that is itself in motion (a prison ship, a rendition plane), since that is reliably off-the-shore of even the offshore territories and not even specifiable in terms of time zone.[6] Remarkably, these offshore territories are at once within the reach of the executive and not within reach of the judiciary, and thus they have just the kind of X / not-X structure—the United States / not the United States—that is needed for constructing an extra-legal universe. The architect will need assistants: if one group is too constrained by laws (as the military usually is), there are others less constrained (the CIA), and still others who have no known legal constraints whatsoever (Blackwater[7]).

The construction of a parallel universe requires that the architect have ample room in which to move. Open-ended spatial zones such the geographical ones just described can also be brought into being by rocking back and forth between two legal categories. Are the terrorists criminals (which would obligate us to pursue them as individuals using criminal law) or state enemies (to be confronted through war)? No need for the architect to choose: he maximizes his freedom by initiating war against two states while designating the villains "non-state actors" ineligible for the protections of the laws of war. We thus fight a not-war war. Small crevices in time also open into new spaces: a seven-day delay in notifying someone whose house has been searched is a window into many previously unenterable rooms; "unlimited detention" without charge of any person named by an executive officer as a terrorist suspect provides unexplored continents of executive maneuverability. Even the weather in this new extra-legal universe will have puzzling features. Would any sensible person complain if it were reported (as it frequently was) that prisoners were being subjected to "air conditioning"? But if a person is subjected to prolonged sleep deprivation, the brain looses its capacity to regulate core body temperature; applications of cold water or cold air, coupled with other techniques, can become lethal.

ELAINE SCARRY   XIX

Written on the eve of the 2008 election, Chapter 3 explains why, even in imagining the best possible outcome—the election of a president who stops torture, closes Guantánamo, gets our soldiers out of Iraq, shifts the trials of detainees to federal courts—the rule of law will not be restored until those officials who licensed torture are prosecuted. A country that tortures when it has a president who believes he is permitted to torture and then abstains from torture when it has a president who recognizes that torture is unconditionally prohibited continues to be a country living under the rule of men, rather than the rule of law; for it is allowing its moral fate to be determined by the personal beliefs of its rulers.

Righting a wrong is especially difficult if the wrong has been initiated by a president. Any occupant of the White House has tremendous charisma, and therefore a tremendous capacity to miseducate. Under the Bush-Cheney administration, some people came to believe that the rules about torture were flexible, conditional, revisable. They were wrong.

That damaging act of miseducation has now almost been corrected. But we have also been miseducated into believing that *the prosecution* of the officials who sanctioned torture is an option, rather than, as is actually the case, a requirement.[8] Both the Geneva Conventions and the Convention Against Torture make prosecution obligatory. When we hear voices coming from inside and from outside the country[9] urging that the United States *must* prosecute, we may mistakenly hear the "must" as expressing the passionate belief of the speaker. It instead reports the legal status of the requirement: like the prohibition on torture, the obligation to prosecute is absolute.

My earlier book, *Who Defended the Country?*, described the inability of the Pentagon to track and bring down Flight 77 even with 55 minutes of warning. It compared this failure with the success of the ordinary citizens on Flight 93 who, in 23 minutes, deliberated, then voted, then acted to bring down their plane before it reached Washington. *Rule of Law, Misrule of Men*, too, is about the population's capacity to defend the country, defensive actions now directed not against invading terrorists but against executive officers who for eight years assaulted the country's laws and, by licensing torture, entered an area of wrongdoing as grave as could ever be entered by a foreign enemy.

1

*Resolving to Resist
(September 2004)*

WHEN, SHORTLY AFTER SEPTEMBER 11, THE U.S.A. Patriot Act first arrived in our midst, its very title seemed to deliver an injury: "Uniting and Strengthening America by Providing Appropriate Tools Required to Intercept and Obstruct Terrorism." The names of the country (U.S.A.) and of those responsible for creating and sustaining it (patriots) had been turned into a Justice Department acronym. One might have thought that "United States of America" would be regarded as a sufficient referent for the letters U.S.A.[1] and that no one would presume to bestow a new set of words on those letters—or attach a new meaning to the word *patriot*, with its heavy freight of history (Paul Revere, Patrick Henry, Emma

Lazarus) and its always fresh aspiration ("O beautiful for patriot dream").

In the two years since its passage by Congress, on October 25, 2001, the U.S.A. Patriot Act has become the locus of resistance against the unceasing injuries of the Bush-Rumsfeld-Ashcroft triumvirate, as first one community, then two, then eleven, then 27, then 238 passed resolutions against it, as have three state legislatures. Many more councils and legislatures have draft resolutions pending. The letters "U.S.A." and the word "patriot" have gradually reacquired their earlier solidity and sufficiency, as local and state governments reanimate the practice of self-rule by opposing the Patriot Act's assault on the personal privacy, free flow of information, and freedom of association that lie at the heart of democracy. Each of the resolutions affirms a town's obligation to uphold the Constitutional rights of all persons who live there, and many of the resolutions explicitly direct police and other residents to refrain from carrying out the provisions of the Patriot Act, even when approached by a federal officer and explicitly instructed to do so.

When the resistance was beginning in the winter of 2001–2002, it took five months for the first five resolutions to come into being; in the winter of 2003–2004, a new resolution comes into being almost every day. The resolutions come from towns ranging from small villages with populations under a thousand—such as Wendell, Massachusetts (986), Riverside, Washington (348), Gaston, Oregon (620), and tiny Crestone, Colorado (73)—to huge cities with populations of many hundreds of thousands—Philadelphia (1,517,550), Baltimore (651,000), Chicago (2,896,000), Detroit (951,000), Austin (656,500), San Francisco (777,000).[2] Approximately one third of the resolutions come from towns and cities with populations between 20,000 and 200,000 people.

That the Patriot Act should became this locus of resistance may at first seem puzzling. True, its legislative history is sordid: it was rushed through Congress in several days; no hearings were held; it went largely unread; only a few of its many egregious provisions were modified. But at least it was passed by Congress; many other blows have been delivered to the people of the United States in the form of unmodified executive edicts, such as the formation of military tribunals and the nullification of attorney-client privilege.[3] True, the Patriot Act severed words from their meanings (beginning with the letters U.S.A.). But executive statements outside the Patriot Act—statements associating Iraq with nuclear weapons and with al Qaeda—have severed words from their basis in material fact, at the very great cost of a war that continues to be mortally destructive. True, the Patriot Act has degraded the legal stature of the United States by permitting the executive branch to bypass Constitutional law. But aren't we so degraded, regardless of the Act? In one area outside the Patriot Act, we appear to have reached rock bottom. Evidence indicates that the Bush administration has created off-shore torture centers in Bagram, Afghanistan (where one prisoner has died of pulmonary embolism, another of a heart attack), and on the British island of Diego Garcia, and has sent prisoners to interrogation centers with documented histories of physical torture in Egypt, Jordan, Saudi Arabia, and Syria.[4]

Each of the enumerated events—the Patriot Act, the executive edicts, the war against Iraq, the alleged practice of torture—has elicited protest from the population. What differentiates the opposition to the Patriot Act from the opposition to the other executive actions is the fact that it is steadily spreading and has gained traction: it has enabled the population to move beyond vocalizing dissent to retarding, and potentially reversing, the executive inclination to carry out actions divorced from the will of the people.

The Patriot Act has become the locus of resistance for three reasons. First, as even the brief summary above suggests, it is continuous with the most extreme actions carried out by the Bush administration. That continuity is visible in the local resolutions, many of which explicitly enumerate, and also carefully distinguish, the Constitutional insults delivered by both the Patriot Act and the executive decrees. Although the executive decrees are by far the most frequently mentioned companions to the Patriot Act, the resolutions also refer to the Homeland Security Act (cited, for example, by Brookline, Massachusetts; Arcata, California; Rockingham, Vermont; Woodstock, New York; and Takoma Park, Maryland), which has one provision arranging for its own exemption from Freedom of Information Act requirements and another arranging for mandatory vaccinations; the not-yet-passed "Patriot Act II" (cited by Astoria, Oregon; Baltimore; Orange County, North Carolina; Reading, Pennsylvania; Rio Arriba, New Mexico; and York, Pennsylvania), which enables the attorney general to strip Americans of their citizenship if he believes they have supported a terrorist group; the attorney general's May 30, 2002, revised guidelines for the FBI (cited by University City, Missouri); the act of taking the country to war in Iraq without a Congressional declaration of war (cited by Blount County, Tennessee); and alleged acts of torture (alluded to by

Bainbridge Island, Washington, which urges that executive practices be tested not only against the U.S. Constitution but against international prohibitions on torture).

Second, the consequences of the Patriot Act are extremely damaging—even considered in isolation from objectionable executive decrees. As the next section shows, they threaten the fundamentals of American democracy, Constitutional protections of noncitizens, and a range of other basic American institutions.

Third, the Patriot Act differs from all the other forms of executive action in one key respect that has proved crucial to the work of resistance: it cannot function without citizen participation. That attribute will be explored in the final section of the essay.

A Structural Injury

If many members of Congress failed to read the Patriot Act during its swift passage, it is in part because the law is almost unreadable. The Patriot Act is written as an extended sequence of additions to and deletions from previously existing statutes. In making these alterations, it often instructs the bewildered reader to insert three words into paragraph X of statute Y without ever providing the full sentence that is altered, either in its original or its amended form. Only someone who had scores of earlier statutes open to the relevant pages could step painstakingly through the revisions. On the issue of electronic surveillance alone, the Patriot Act modifies the Electronic Communications Privacy Act, the Foreign Intelligence Surveillance Act, the Cable Act, the Federal Wiretap Statutes, and the Federal Rules of Criminal Procedure. Reading the Patriot Act is like being forced to spend the night on the steps outside the public library, trying to infer the sentences in the books inside by listening to hundreds of mice chewing away on the pages.[5]

The hundreds of additions and deletions do, despite appearances, have a coherent and unitary direction: many of them increase the power of the

Justice Department and decrease the rights of individual persons.[6] The Constitutional rights abridged by the Patriot Act are enumerated in the town resolutions, which most often specify violations of the First Amendment guarantee of free speech and assembly, the Fourth Amendment guarantee against search and seizure, the Fifth and Fourteenth Amendment guarantees of due process, and (cited somewhat less often) the Sixth and Eighth Amendment guarantees of a speedy and public trial and protection against cruel and unusual punishment.

The unifying work of the Patriot Act is even clearer if, rather than summarizing it as an increase in the power of the Justice Department and a corresponding decrease in the rights of persons, it is understood concretely as making the population *visible* and the Justice Department *invisible*.

The Patriot Act inverts the Constitutional requirement that people's lives be private and the work of government officials be public; it instead crafts a set of conditions in which our inner lives become transparent, and the workings of the government become opaque. Either one of these outcomes would imperil democracy; together they not only injure the country but also cut off the avenues of repair.

When we say that democracy requires that the people's privacy be ensured, we do not mean that our lives remain secret; we mean instead that we individually control the degree to which, and the people to whom, our inner lives are revealed.[7] From *Griswold v. Connecticut* (1965) to *Lawrence v. Texas* (2003), the Supreme Court has affirmed that privacy is a fundamental Constitutional value and located its roots in the First, Third, Fourth, and Fifth Amendments. In an elegant summary of the underlying theory, Constitutional scholar Kenneth Karst has argued that privacy has a three-part architecture. Privacy means first of all "informational privacy"—control over personal information and judgments. Such privacy is in turn the basis of a person's capacity for friendship and intimacy. Lastly it is the foundation of moral autonomy and liberty, since freedom is premised on making important decisions based on independent judgment.[8] Inhabitants of a country who lose the guarantee of privacy also eventually lose the capacity for making friends and the capacity for political freedom.[9]

As necessary to democracy as this non-transparency of persons is the transparency of government actions. Because we have, for the past three decades, focused so intensely on the Constitutional guarantee of personal privacy but not on the corresponding requirement of the non-privacy (or publicness, or publication) of the acts of governors, it is useful now to recall how many times the Constitution pauses to require the act of creating of an open record: "Each house [of Congress] shall keep a Journal of its Proceedings, and from time to time publish the same" with "the Yeas and Nays of the Members . . . entered on the Journal" (Article I, Section 5);[10] a roll-call vote, recording not just numbers but names, is required when Congress overrides a presidential veto (I, 7); "a regular Statement and Account of the Receipts and Expenditures of all public Money shall be published from time to time" (I, 9); presidential objections to a piece of legislation must be forwarded to the house in which the legislation originated and published in their journal (I, 7); every Congressional vote, with the exception of a vote on adjournment, "shall be presented to the President" (I, 7); the counting of the Electoral College votes must take place in the presence of the full Congress (II, 1; Amendment 12); the president is authorized to require the "opinion in writing, of the principal Officer in each of the executive Departments" (II, 2); the president "shall from time to time give to the Congress Information of the State of the Union, and recommend to their Consideration such Measures as he shall judge necessary and expedient" (II, 3); treason proceedings will take place in "open Court" (III, 3) and criminal prosecutions in a "public trial" (Amendment 6).[11] Unlike Article I (on the Congress) and Article II (on the presidency), Article III (on the courts) does not specify the keeping of records; but the assumption of open record-keeping is indicated by the opening clause of Article IV (on the states): "Full Faith and Credit shall be given in each State to the public Acts, Records and judicial Proceedings of every other state."

The obligation of each branch to make its actions public—to make them visible both to the population and to the other branches—is often construed as a right belonging to the population, the right of access to information or "freedom of information," and is closely bound up with First Amendment protections of free speech. Though scholars and jurists disagree about the extent to which access to government information is guaranteed by the Constitution (as well as by subsequent legislative acts, particularly the Freedom of Information Act of 1966 and the later 1972–1978 statutes), it is hard to disagree with the stark argument—made with particular force by Alexander Meiklejohn and Cass Sunstein—that democratic deliberation is impossible without this access to information: "If information is kept secret, public deliberation cannot occur." Secrecy, continues Sunstein, "is inconsistent with self-rule." Or, as the local resolution of Astoria, Oregon, recently phrased it, "Secrecy . . . undermines established norms for civil discourse between government and those it would govern." Sunstein identifies citizen deliberation as the primary benefit of open government, but he also identifies other benefits, including "checks and balances" (one branch cannot check the other if it does not know what the other is doing), "deterrence" (national security may actually be strengthened by revelation of the country's resources), and "sunlight as disinfectant" (if deliberations are carried out in secret, "participants may be less careful to ensure their behavior is unaffected by illegitimate or irrelevant considerations").[12]

The double requirement—that people's lives be private and government actions be public—is turned inside out by the Patriot Act. The inner lives of people are made involuntarily transparent by provisions that increase the ability of officers of the executive branch to enter and search a person's house (section 213); to survey private medical records, business records, library records, and educational records (sections 203, 215, 218, 219, 358, 507, 508);[13] and to monitor telephone, email, and Internet use (section 216). Simultaneously, the Patriot Act obscures executive-branch actions, hiding those actions from the population and from the legislative and judicial branches, and doing so before, during, and after the executive actions are carried out. One provision lowers the standards for "probable cause" (the need to show the courts evidence of a crime) to monitor a phone or computer, thereby almost releasing the executive branch from judicial supervision, a key feature of Constitutional checks and balances (section 216). Another provision releases the government from the obligation to inform a person that her house is about to be searched; it permits delayed notification of seven days and continual postponement thereafter (section 213). Another provision releases the CIA from its obligation to submit intelligence reports to Congress, instead allowing the secretary of defense, the attorney general, or the CIA director to defer the date of reporting (section 904).

ELAINE SCARRY   15

The goal of making the actions of the executive branch opaque is carried out not only by the content of the Patriot Act, but by its form—its lengthy and barely comprehensible list of revisions to scores of previously existing laws. The Patriot Act empowers the executive branch while obscuring the features of that empowerment. Some of the 238 local resolutions focus explicitly on the Patriot Act's unwieldy form: Blount County, Tennessee, observes that it contains 1,016 sections; Philadelphia and San Mateo, California, both note its extensive page length; Philadelphia registers the absence of Congressional hearings or markup sessions during its rapid passage;[14] Amherst, Massachusetts, complains that it was "passed hurriedly"; and the Alaskan city of North Pole observes that such "sweeping legislation required intense public review and comment before it was passed." Librarians and other ardent readers have recognized from the outset the importance of making the Act lucid and have therefore played a pivotal role in the resistance to it, a subject I return to later.

The content of the Patriot Act is the principal concern, however. And while it may look like a ticker tape of tiny revisions in the phrasing of previous laws, that content goes to the core of our political life: it distorts not just this or that particular feature of governance but the basic act of self-governance itself. Because the privacy of individual action and the publication of government action are both necessary to democratic self-rule (that is, to the debate, deliberation, and decision-making on which self-rule is premised), the major complaint of the local resolutions concerns the damage done to the liberties of persons and to the integrity of our laws. The most high-keyed formulation of this worry comes at the conclusion of Blount County's resolution, which calls on all residents to study the U.S. Constitution so that they can resist not only the executive acts that have already been formulated but those that may come in the days ahead: "to study the Bill of Rights so that they can recognize and resist attempts to undermine our Constitutional Republic . . . and declare null and void all future attempts to establish Martial Law, [or] Declared States of Emergency."[15] While most of the other 237 local resolutions are more measured in their language, the documents consistently register the view that both the people and the laws of the country are endangered. Together the local resolutions constitute a treatise on self-governance and the rule of law.

Justice for All

The resolutions have a second, closely related focus. Though the Patriot Act—in the words of the Boulder, Colorado resolution—increases the federal government's power "to detain and investigate citizens and non-citizens," and to carry out "surveillance of citizens and non-citizens," its blows fall most heavily on those who are not U.S. citizens.

Consider section 412. As summarized by the city of Ann Arbor, it permits the incarceration of noncitizens for seven days without charge, and "for six month periods indefinitely without access to counsel" if the attorney general "determines release would endanger either the country or individual persons." Before it was modified by Congress, the attorney general's draft of the Patriot Act allowed for the unlimited detention of immigrants, rather than a seven-day period. But the Congressional revision is less of an improvement than it at first appears, since various loopholes release the executive branch from the seven-day constraint. As Michael T. McCarthy observes,

> The effect of the U.S.A. Patriot Act . . . is to allow the Attorney General to detain indefinitely not only those convicted of crimes or immigration offenses . . . but also any person the Attorney General has reasonable grounds to believe is a terrorist or is engaged in any other activity that endangers the national security.

Resolutions such as those of Detroit, Seattle, Minneapolis, and the California cities of Pinole, Oakland, Richmond, and San Francisco observe that among those most at risk are persons of Muslim, Middle

Eastern, or South Asian descent. The Chicago resolution also describes the risks to Latinos.

The resolutions collectively work to prevent this imperilment of all residents of the United States. Almost without exception, the 238 resolutions celebrate their commitment to law and liberty for all "persons" or "residents," not only "citizens."

This celebration is expressed in part as a matter of Constitutional conviction. The first clause of the very first resolution (Ann Arbor) echoes the 2001 Supreme Court decision in *Zadvydas v. Davis*: "Whereas, the due process and equal protection clauses of the 5th and 14th Amendments to the United States Constitution guarantee certain due process and equal rights to all residents of the United States, regardless of citizenship or immigration status . . ."[16] The Cambridge, Massachusetts resolution explicitly cites the Zadvydas case.

Other resolutions remind all residents of a matter of political principle: discrimination based on "citizenship status" is no more permissible than discrimination based on race or gender. And many resolutions found their concerns on civic solidarities or on the public contributions of noncitizens. They complain that the Patriot Act tries "to drive a wedge" between citizens and noncitizens, or between police and residents, or between police and foreign nationals, a situation held to be intolerable because the town depends on the diverse population for its "vitality" and its "economy, culture, and civic character" (Arlington, Massachusetts and Aztec and Rio Arriba, New Mexico, respectively). Individual resolutions give specific reasons why the presence of foreign nationals, vital to all localities, is especially life-giving to this particular place: it may be because the town is tiny and therefore depends on each and every one of its residents (the reason given by Castle Valley, Utah); because both foreign students and workers reside there (York, Pennsylvania; University City, Missouri; Arlington, Massachusetts; and Flagstaff, Arizona); because it is a port city (Baltimore); or because foreign nationals living within the city already have the right to vote in municipal elections (Takoma Park, Maryland).

Almost the only time "citizens" are singled out is when one of the documents—such as those of Philadelphia; San Jose, Washington; and Amherst, Massachusetts—places on "citizens" the burden of acting to ensure that all "persons" or "residents" enjoy the benefits of due process, protection from unwarranted search and seizure, and freedom of speech, assembly, and privacy. If, in other words, citizens are unique, it is because they are the guardians of rights belonging to citizens and noncitizens alike, not the exclusive holders of those rights.

More Damage

In addition to aiming blows at our legal framework of self-governance and our political convictions about protecting both citizens and noncitizens, the Patriot Act licenses the executive branch to harm other institutions, such as financial markets and universities. Once again, its blows appear to be structural, to go to the foundations of these institutions.

Take, for example, section 356, which requires bankers, broker-dealers, commodity merchants, and trading advisers to file "suspicious activity reports" (SARs) when they notice their clients carrying out unusual actions that entail the transfer of more than $5,000. In the past, the filing of such reports was voluntary, and the guidelines stipulated $100,000, not $5,000, as the triggering sum. Today the act of filing is mandatory. Failure to file is punishable by criminal and civil charges, with fines reaching $10,000.[17] Furthermore, one is prohibited from telling one's client about the SAR, which not only taints one's relationship with that client but eliminates at the outset the possibility of determining whether the transfer of money has some sensible explanation that, if known, would demonstrate the preposterousness of filing. The Patriot Act seeks to enlist the financial community into its intelligence-gathering operation not only by penalizing individuals who fail to file but by immunizing those who do. The Act provides a "safe harbor" for the filer.[18] Should an innocent person become the subject of a SAR and subsequently suffer harm as a result, the person who filed the report cannot be held liable.

You do not have to be a banker or a trading adviser or a commodity merchant or one of their clients to see a problem here—a problem that, at least from the outside, looks less like a decorative inflection in the practice of those markets than a foundational strike at the structure of trust, privacy, good faith, and the assumption of innocence without which markets cannot operate.

Universities, too, are among the institutions the Patriot Act seeks to change, and again we may ask the question: is the alteration superficial or structural? The situation may be swiftly assessed by looking at the two spaces that stand most directly in the path of damage: the library and the laboratory. Not the side paths, not the attic, not the bell tower, not the kitchen, not the playing fields, but the heart of the sciences (the laboratory) and the arts (the library).

Section 817 of the Patriot Act lists "restricted persons" who henceforth are not allowed to work in the presence of specified biological and chemical materials. Legal and illegal aliens from countries that, in the judgment of the secretary of state, support terrorism (Cuba, Iran, Iraq, Libya, North Korea, Syria, Sudan) are placed in the company of convicted criminals and persons determined to be "mentally defective" and prohibited from contact with even the paper record of listed substances. At first, the list of named substances included almost no materials used in campus laboratories. But as MIT, among other institutions, correctly anticipated, the list of biological and chemical substances would soon grow longer, as would the list of foreign nationals prohibited from entering the laboratory.[19]

In a lucid, publicly available report, MIT described "the growing pressure to . . . create a new landscape for faculty, students, and MIT as an institution."[20] The new landscape would be built on a two-tiered system consisting of two categories of people: one that could pass freely in and out of the space of education and another that could not. That outcome would starkly revise MIT's own research policy, which specifies that no research requiring "classification on process, funding, or results" can take place on campus without approval by the university's provost; since 1975 no such approval has been granted.[21] The faculty report observes that a legislative act which obligates an institution "to identify and prevent 'restricted persons' from having access to specific classified agents" threatens to change the campus in almost the same way that the traditional category of "classified research" does.[22] The report urges that MIT decline all research that would place the university in the position of building two-tiered spaces anywhere on campus. Many other universities have voiced similar concern.

As with the laboratories, so with the libraries (both university and public). No section of the Patriot Act has been so widely discussed as section 215, which applies to (though it does not name) both college and public libraries (and, in many cases, bookstores). When approached by an FBI or CIA agent, librarians must turn over a record of the books a specified patron has taken out. The librarian—like the banker who files a suspicious activity report—is not permitted to tell anyone of the intelligence gathering in which he or she has just participated: "No person shall disclose to any other person (other than those persons necessary to produce the tangible things under this section) that the Federal Bureau of Investigation has sought or obtained tangible things under this section." When the Patriot Act was rolling through the empty corridors of Congress in the middle of the anthrax panic, the American Library Association inhabited those hallways, too, trying valiantly to introduce an amendment that would exempt libraries from the reach of the act.[23] But according to the American Library Association's own account, it could not even get accurate records of the wording of either the House or the Senate versions of the Act and had to rely on "rumor."[24]

Anyone should know not to get on the wrong side of librarians, and the Bush administration must, in retrospect, ardently wish the American Library Association had gotten its exemption; for soon after the passage of the bill and while the rest of the country was still scratching its head, only dimly aware that there was such a thing as the Patriot Act, notices began appearing in local newspapers all over the country, announcing "A Lecture to be Held on the Patriot Act" at this or that town library and describing the deep dilemma in which the always-conscientious librarians now found themselves.[25] In his September 2003 tour of sixteen cities to defend the Patriot Act, Attorney General John Ashcroft dismissed the idea that the Justice Department could conceivably care about librarians or library records, an act of jeering that echoed the earlier derision of FBI officers.[26]

The derision is puzzling since it seems to imply that librarians do not have any history of serving as political actors, an implication starkly at odds with national and international history.[27] More to the point, and perhaps as a result of their lack of interest in libraries, the attorney general and his assistants appear not to have read a University of Illinois study which found that by February of 2002 (four months after the Patriot Act was passed) 4 percent of all U.S. libraries, and 11 percent of all libraries in communities of more than 50,000 people had already been visited by FBI agents requesting information about their patrons' reading habits.[28] Attorney General Ashcroft then indignantly insisted that not-yet-released FBI records would demonstrate the indifference of the Justice Department to the libraries, but the Justice Department had for the preceding two years refused to release these very same records, despite Freedom of Information Act petitions filed by the American Civil Liberties Union, the Freedom to Read Foundation, and the Electronic Privacy Information Center.[29]

Earlier it was observed that if a government obscures the record of its own activity while forcing the population into transparency, it not only injures democracy but also cuts off the path of repair. We can see how this works in the case of libraries. Stated in distilled form, the logic of the Patriot Act and its defense involves five steps:

- Maximize the power of the Justice Department.

- Erase the public record of Justice Department actions.

- Respond with indignation if anyone protests that the Justice Department might actually be using its newly expanded powers.

- Point out that the protesters are speaking without any hard evidence or facts (without mentioning that the executive branch has withheld those very facts from the public).

- If necessary, pull out a piece of previously withheld "evidence" that shows the Justice Department knows more than the foolish protesters.[30]

This formula has by no means defeated Patriot Act–resistance in the long run, but it has deterred it, by giving an individual who recognizes the dangers the law poses to the country only two choices: step forward and speak without complete evidence in hand (and risk being jeered at by federal officers or even by one's own community) or be silent—in other words, either immediate self-silencing or slightly delayed silencing-by-others. Take the case of Bill Olds, who used to write a regular column about civil liberties for *The Hartford Courant*. When he learned from local librarians that FBI officers had (without giving any explanation) walked into the library, seized the hard drive of a computer, and then walked out again, he began to complain in print about section 215 of the Patriot Act and the seizure of private records. The local FBI office, swollen with indignation at the suggestion that it might actually do what the Patriot Act allowed it to, announced self-righteously that the officers had seized the computer because they were on the track of an alleged ordinary criminal, not an alleged terrorist.[31] Both the *Courant* and Olds were embarrassed by the episode, and Olds lost his job.[32]

It is crucial that the concrete record of actual abuses carried out by the executive branch under section 215, as well as many other sections of the Patriot Act, be made public. But the record of its use should not deflect attention from the reprehensible quality of the

Patriot Act itself. From the founding of this country the phrase "a government of laws and not of men" has always meant that the country cannot pass open-ended laws that will be good if the governors happen to be good, and bad if the governors happen to be bad. The goal has always been to pass laws that will protect everyone regardless of the temperament and moral character of the individual governors. The country, as Justice David Davis famously observed in 1866, "has no right to expect that it will always have wise and humane rulers." That is why it is crucial to pass good laws. And crucial, also, to repeal bad ones.

Resistance

Despite impediments to resistance, 238 towns, cities, and counties have now created a firewall against executive trespass in their communities. Though there are many differences among the resolutions, the resistance is built out of six identifiable acts, the first five of which require little explanation, while the sixth requires fuller attention.

Clarify. The resolutions describe the Constitutional provisions that are violated, the specific sections of the Patriot Act through which the violations occur, the relation between the Patriot Act and other executive extensions of power, and who is at risk. In their clarity they undo the cringing obscurity of the Act itself. The resolutions are distributed through local publications and postings: the Brookline, Massachusetts resolution, for example, explicitly calls on "the Town Clerk and the Board of Selectmen jointly [to] endeavor to publish this resolution and post it in public places, e.g., kiosks, bulletin boards, and the lobbies of Town Hall, the libraries and public schools . . ."[33]

Warn. The act of clarifying alerts town residents to the dangers of violating the act and therefore itself constitutes a form of warning. In addition, some of the resolutions—such as those of Oxford, Ohio; Baltimore; Detroit; Newton, Massachusetts; and Rio Arriba and Aztec, New Mexico—explicitly provide for a sign warning residents about section 215 in the town library:

The City of Aztec . . . DIRECTS public libraries within the City of Aztec to post in a prominent place within the library a notice to library users as follows:

WARNING: under Section 215 of the federal USA PATRIOT Act (Public Law 107-56), records of the books and other materials you borrow from this library may be obtained by federal agents. That federal law prohibits librarians from informing you if federal agents have obtained records about you. Questions about this policy should be directed to: Attorney General John Ashcroft, Department of Justice, Washington, DC 20530.[34]

The presence of a warning sign in libraries in turn inspires people to post warnings in other spaces not explicitly cited in the resolutions: banks, brokerage firms, medical offices, computer labs.

A Call for Reporting. Many resolutions call upon the executive branch (including local FBI and U.S. Attorney offices) to report to the town the number and names of residents detained or imprisoned and to specify the number of library records, medical records, business records, or emails that have been monitored.[35] The resolutions usually specify a time interval, conveying to the federal government their expectation that they will receive reports "monthly" (Ithaca, New York; Orleans, Massachusetts), "every three months" (Lane County, Oregon), "every six months" (Rio Arriba, New Mexico), or "regularly and publicly" (Guilford, Burlington, Jamaica, Marlboro, Putney, and Athens, Vermont; Northampton, Leverett, Provincetown, and Eastham, Massachusetts; Madison, Wisconsin; Davis and Mendocino, California; Broward County, Florida; Takoma Park, Maryland; and New Paltz, New York).[36] Though the town and city resolutions cannot make the federal government comply, the call for reporting reinstates and places on the record the expectation of transparency in government actions. It thereby delivers a warning to the federal government.

Repeal. Many localities—Chicago; Minneapolis; Ithaca, New York; Burlington, Vermont; Corvallis, Oregon; Eastham and Northampton, Massachusetts;

Fairfax, California, and scores of others—call upon their Congressional representatives to repeal the sections of the Patriot Act that violate the Constitutional rights of residents.[37] Defenders of the Patriot Act sometimes argue that the urgency of repeal is mitigated by the "sunset clause," which shuts down the act on December 31, 2005. But far from cutting off the effects of the Patriot Act, the sunset clause explicitly permits all investigations of international terrorism already underway as of December 31, 2005, to continue indefinitely.

Unite. Each resident is, side by side with all other residents, constitutive of the town, city, or county; and all residents are, regardless of citizenship, bearers of rights. Hence, "a threat to any one person's Constitutional rights is a threat to the rights of all" (a principle stated in the Philadelphia, Duluth, and Amherst, Massachusetts, resolutions). The asymmetry between citizen and foreign national lies in the citizen's greater obligation to uphold the Constitution and to protect "the rights of all people, including

United States citizens and citizens of other nations, living within the City."

Decline to Assist. The resolutions direct the town police, town employees, and residents to decline to assist the federal government in any act that violates the U.S. Constitution. Local police should abstain from assisting federal officers in house searches that violate the Fourth Amendment (the police and town councils often work together to find the wording for the instructions that will be most helpful to police). Likewise, librarians should abstain from giving out private library records in a manner that violates the First and Fourth Amendments, and bankers should abstain from filing suspicious activity reports for the same reason.[38]

Because federal officers cannot carry out their acts of trespass without the assistance of police, bankers, and librarians, the refusal of police, bankers, and librarians to assist provides a concrete brake on federal action. It brings them to a halt. Hence, unlike the third and fourth acts of resistance (the calls for reporting and for repeal), this sixth act carries the power of its own enforcement.

Here we have the key to why the Patriot Act—rather than the executive edicts—has become the locus of resistance. In actions in which the general population's participation is not needed, the general population's approval or disapproval is a matter of indifference to the executive. Since military tribunals do not require the assistance of the population, military tribunals are not ours to assist or to decline to assist; hence what we think about the military tribunals is a matter of indifference to the executive. Since the country has a standing army rather than a draft, the general population's assistance is not needed to fight foreign wars; to our great peril, the war against Iraq was neither ours to assist nor to decline to assist. The executive branch can carry out alleged acts of torture without the people's help, so neither its approval of nor its hostility to such acts is of any interest to the executive. If, without the population's assistance, 5,000 foreign nationals can be detained without charges (only four of whom were, in the end, charged with terrorism-related acts),[39] then the population's disapproval of this detention is like smoke rings in the wind.

But the aspirations encoded in the Patriot Act—the making transparent of the population and the making invisible of the executive branch—cannot be fulfilled without the help of people everywhere. While (in other words) the actions of our executive branch have, like a runaway train, become divorced from the will of the people, here in the Patriot Act the government is still dependent upon its people, and therefore the population can exert, and is exerting, a braking power. The problem is not that we—local librarians, or police, or bankers—are being asked to assist: a government and its people must be yoked together in a democracy, and the many areas in which they have become unyoked need to be repaired. The problem is being asked to assist in acts defying the Constitution and betraying our country.

People sometimes say the Patriot Act has become the locus of resistance for selfish reasons: here, not just foreign nationals but U.S. citizens are among those at risk, and therefore a groundswell of opposition has arisen. If this is true, it is only partially true, for—as noted earlier—the legal rights of foreign nationals are a major subject of the resolutions (beginning with the first "whereas" clause of the first town resolution passed). Furthermore, there is nothing illegitimate about acting out of self-interest: democracy puts the levers of government in the hands of the people in part because they can best judge what is in their own interest. But more important than self-interest[40] in explaining why the Patriot Act has become the locus of resistance is that, with this act, people everywhere stand to become not just the victims of executive action but assistants to its injuries; apparently, people in the United States have a strong aversion to betraying their Constitution and their neighbors.

The executive's request for assistance bears considerable resemblance to the Writs of Assistance that preceded the American Revolution. The Writs, issued by the British king, enabled royal officers in Boston Harbor to search houses at will for smuggled goods.[41] The Fourth Amendment was designed to make the Writs impossible:

> The right of the people to be secure in their persons, houses, papers, and effects, against unreasonable searches and seizures, shall not be violated, and no Warrants shall issue, *but upon probable cause*, supported by Oath or affirmation, and *particularly describing the place to be searched, and the persons or things to be seized*. (Emphasis added.)

The Patriot Act violates the Fourth Amendment; like the Writs, the Patriot Act is a gigantic license to search and seize. As previously mentioned, it explicitly lowers the probable cause requirement (section 216), thereby also diminishing judicial review. Equally important, the Patriot Act eliminates the specificity clause—"particularly describing the place to be searched, and the persons or things to be seized"—which, like probable cause, places severe restraints on the scope and duration of the search. Far from specifying the place to be searched and the persons or things to be seized, the Patriot Act is a many-page-long permission slip to search and seize everywhere and anywhere guided not by court-validated standards of evidence but by Justice department hunches and racially inflected intuitions.

The Patriot Act resembles the Writs of Assistance not only in its dilution of probable cause and in its perilous lack of specificity but also in a third key feature: it permits officers of the executive branch to conscript residents and passersby into assisting in the search. Opposition to the Writs—which began with a fiery speech by James Otis in a Massachusetts courtroom—was credited by John Adams with igniting the American Revolution: "there," Adam's wrote, "the child Independence was born."[42]

The grass-roots aversion to being conscripted into the sweeping intelligence-gathering measures of the Patriot Act coincides with the verdict reached in a pre-9/11 Fourth Amendment case in which a by-stander was enlisted into a police action. Judge Jon Blue of the Connecticut Superior Court ruled that the act of unwarranted "seizure" applies not just to a person arrested without warrant but also to a person forced to assist: "It is a misuse of power in modern society for an agent of the state to . . . draft a citizen off the street and impress him into [hazardous duty]. Our security does not demand that the government be given such a power."[43]

Judge Blue was speaking about physically hazardous police duty, but his words appear to apply as well to morally hazardous police duty that involves abridging the rights of fellow residents. Librarians, local police, bankers, brokers, and physicians all stand in danger of being subject to an act of seizure by the federal government.

Sorting out the Writs of Assistance in the pre-Revolutionary period took time: though their tyrannical and invasive power would in the long run be curtailed by the creation of a new country armed with the Fourth Amendment, the short run was not without setbacks. Otis lost the case in which he made the speech that so inspired Adams and others around Boston Harbor. Otis was physically beaten by royalists and, according to his sister, eventually died from those wounds.[44]

Sorting out the legal status of the Patriot Act's writs of assistance may also take time. Though the Constitution prohibits acts that the Patriot Act licenses, and though the Patriot Act's lack of legislative history may invalidate it as a "piece of legislation," for the time being it appears to empower the federal government not only to call on the country's residents for assistance but—as in the case of the suspicious activity reports—to impose criminal and civil penalties on those who fail to comply.

If two legal provisions conflict, one of them Constitutional and one legislative, the Constitutional provision takes precedence, a principle reiterated throughout the resolutions. Scores of towns and cities remind their employees that their first obligation is to the Constitution; in the words of San Juan, Washington, "the paramount responsibility of local law enforcement personnel, and appointed and elected government offices" is to follow "the solemn oath they have taken to preserve, uphold, protect, and defend the Constitution of the United States and the State of Washington Constitution." Many resolutions express confidence that defending the United States against terrorism is compatible with a rigorous standard of civil liberties, and some call attention to the fact that the Constitution and the Bill of Rights, far from being premised on peace, were themselves written against a background of bloodshed. Some resolutions skillfully elaborate the primacy of Constitutional law over statutory law: Oroville, Washington, for example, cites Article 6 of the Constitution, which requires laws and treaties to be made in conformity with the Constitution; it also cites the *Marbury v. Madison* ruling: "All laws which are repugnant to the Constitution are null and void."

But until Congress repeals the Patriot Act, or until a court rules it unconstitutional, resisters may be vulnerable to federal penalties or detention that the rest of us may not even hear about.[45] The 238 resolutions collectively register the legal complexity of the refusal to assist. The guidelines they provide fall into three distinguishable tiers. One set of resolutions states that public employees (or in some cases, both employees and residents) should continue to uphold Constitutional rights. A second set of resolutions is more explicit: city officials should continue to uphold Constitutional rights and decline to assist the federal government, even if asked. Within this second set, some towns and cities flatly recommend declining assistance whereas others stipulate that officials should "decline assistance as far as it is legally possible to do so." A third set—consisting at present of at least one town, Arcata, California—is yet more explicit: residents should decline to assist any act that entails violating a fellow resident's Constitutional rights, and the town itself will cover the resister's legal expenses, should the federal government try to impose a criminal charge. Arcata was the first place to pass an ordinance prohibiting employees from "assisting or voluntarily co-operating."

To be sure, trouble may lie ahead: even if the courts issue a ruling, the initial ruling may not uphold the resisters. A number of the resolutions prepare for the eventuality of a negative ruling by explicitly stipulating that if a court invalidates any phrase or clause of the resolution, the rest of the resolution remains in force (Gaston, Oregon; Lane County, Oregon; Lansdowne, Pennsylvania; New Haven, Connecticut; Amherst, Massachusetts; Madison, Wisconsin; the July 2003 supplement to Ann Arbor's January 2002 resolution; Arcata, California).

So far, however, both Congress and the courts appear to be listening attentively (and not punitively). Members of Congress have initiated bills to nullify or limit specific provisions of the Patriot Act. In July 2003 the House passed an amendment to the 2004 Appropriations Bill that withholds all federal funding from section 213 (the provision that allows the Justice Department to search a house without notifying the resident). The sudden disappearance of federal funding will (if also passed by the Senate and if the House and Senate together override a presidential veto) increase the executive branch's reliance on local cooperation for carrying out section 213, the very thing the local resolutions promise to withhold. If Attorney General Ashcroft's August 2003 visit to sixteen cities was motivated by any single event, it was surely this surprising withdrawal by the House of federal funding from the "sneak and peak" provision of the Patriot Act;[46] it was almost the first time since 9/11 that the executive branch felt it needed to make a case for itself to the population.[47] While the Justice Department has tried to portray resistance to the Patriot Act as a liberal complaint, the resisters repeatedly describe themselves as occupying positions across the political spectrum. The amendment to stop funding section 213, for example, was introduced by the conservative Republican Butch Otter of Idaho. Passed by a vote of 309 to 118, it was affirmed by "almost all Democrats and more than half of all Republicans."[48]

Legislative initiatives now pending in the Senate include the "Protecting the Rights of Individuals Act," which proposes the most comprehensive modifications of the Patriot Act;[49] the SAFE Act, which exempts librarians from section 215, narrows the Justice Department's access to other records under 215, restricts federal use of the sneak-and-peak provision, and increases the probable cause requirement for surveillance);[50] the "Patriot Oversight Restoration Act," which subjects previously exempt provisions to the sunset clause unless Congress, upon reviewing them, explicitly acts to renew them;[51] the "Domestic Surveillance Oversight Act," which requires the Justice Department to increase its level of reporting to Congress about the use, under the Patriot Act, of the Foreign Intelligence Surveillance Act;[52] the "Library, Bookseller, and Personal Records Privacy Act," which makes it harder for the executive branch to obtain the records of a person's reading habits or business transactions using section 215 of the Patriot Act;[53] and the "Restoration of Freedom of Information Act," which returns to the population its right to obtain information about the government's activities, temporarily lost under the Homeland Security Act and potentially lost forever under Patriot Act II.[54]

Often when legislators introduce these proposed changes, they directly credit the localities. In October 2003, for example, Congress began a series of hearings to assess executive branch actions under the Patriot Act. The hearings opened with a salute to the localities by Senator Patrick Leahy—who noted what was, by late October, 190 local resolutions in 34 states—and by Senator Ted Kennedy—who observed, "Rarely in recent years have the activities of the Justice Department been so often at the forefront of public discussion, so controversial, and so much in need of public scrutiny."[55] The House vote defeating funding for section 213 was described by Congressman Dennis Kucinich as a direct response to the local resolutions: "This action spoke to the anxiety of millions of Americans who believe the Patriot Act must be repealed or revised to restore fundamental civil liberties to this nation."[56] New legislation dreamed up by the Justice Department now either never reaches the floor of Congress (as is so far true of Patriot Act II)[57] or, if brought there, is soundly defeated (the unanimous Senate vote in early July 2003 to defeat the Pentagon plan for cyber-surveillance entitled "Total Information Awareness").

Recent court actions also echo the concerns of the local resolutions. In the first two years after 9/11, the federal courts appeared to support the executive branch: they tended to issue rulings that upheld executive actions or else to decline cases that contested them.[58] But in December 2003 two federal courts—the Second Circuit U.S. Court of Appeals in New York and the Ninth Circuit in California—issued rulings declaring acts of detention carried out by the Bush administration unlawful.[59] Though they did not address the legality of the Patriot Act, the courts objected to executive branch actions on the same grounds voiced throughout the town resolutions: the violation of separation of powers[60] and the denial of due process to citizens and noncitizens alike.[61] Like the local resolutions, the two courts acknowledged the real dangers of terrorism while insisting that it is by preserving structures of governance (separation of powers and civil liberties), not by suspending them, that terrorism will be defeated.[62] In late January 2004 a federal court in Los Angeles ruled one section of the Patriot Act unconstitutional: the judge objected to the provision making it a crime to provide "expert advice and assistance" to terrorists on the ground that the phrasing is so vague as to give the Justice Department license to interfere with First Amendment speech guarantees. How the courts will rule in the future is, of course, not clear.

In advance of these crucial, but far from final, acts by Congress and the courts is the steady, confident spread of the local resolutions. As noted at the outset, beginning in the winter of 2001–2002, it took five months for the first five resolutions to come into being; in the winter of 2003–2004, five or more new resolutions are approved almost every week. Whether the resistance to the Patriot Act gains more and more momentum or instead gets derailed, the town resolutions remind us that the power of enforcement lies not just with local police but with all those who reside in cities, towns, villages, isolated byways, and country lanes. Law—whether local, state, federal, or Constitutional—is only real if, in the words of Patrick Henry, the rest of us will "put our hands to it, put our hearts to it, stand behind it."

After hearing a speech by Georgetown Law Professor David Cole detailing the many ways in which immigrants in this country have been brutalized since 9/11, a frustrated audience member asked, "There must be a law or a Constitutional provision that can stop this! What is it? What is the thing that can constrain Bush and Ashcroft?" Cole repeated the question and answered it: "What is the thing that can constrain Bush and Ashcroft? We are."

2

*Rules of Engagement
(November 2006)*

IN 1998 AN ARTICLE BY COLONEL CHARLES J. Dunlap Jr. appeared in the United States Air Force Academy's *Journal of Legal Studies* warning that a new form of warfare lay ahead. Because American military resources are so far beyond those of any other country, Dunlap argued, no society can today meet it through symmetric warfare. Therefore, the United States's 21st-century opponents will stop confronting it with weapons and rules that are the mirror counterparts of its own. They will instead use asymmetric or "neo-absolutist" forms of warfare, resorting to unconventional weapons and to procedures forbidden by international laws.

What Dunlap meant by "unconventional weapons" is clear: not only outlawed biological, chemical, and nuclear weapons (the last of which, in the view of the United States, only itself and a small number of other countries are legally permitted to have), but also unexpected weapons such as civilian passenger planes loaded with fuel and flown into towering buildings in densely populated cities.

However, the term "neo-absolutism," as used by Dunlap, applies not just to the use of unconventional weapons but to conduct that violates a sacrosanct set of rules—acts that are categorically prohibited by international law and by the regulations of the U.S. Air Force, Navy, and Army (along with the military forces of many other nations). For example, though warfare permits many forms of ruse and deception, it never permits the false use of a white flag of truce or a red cross. The white flag and red cross—along with a tiny number of other symbols and rules—are held to be inviolable, and their intentional misuse is regarded by the laws of nations as "perfidy," and, when employed to injure or kill, "treachery." A memorable example of such treachery occurred during the spring 2003 invasion of Iraq by the United States, when an Iraqi taxi driver allegedly displayed a white flag at a checkpoint and then, having gained the trust of the guards, exploded a car bomb, killing four American soldiers.[1] Though Iraqi forces were at that moment being attacked by American equipment whose power to injure was in vast excess of anything owned by the Iraqis, media in the United States and around the world rightly paused to express horror and indignation at the deceptive use of a white flag, as they would again pause to express horror a few months later when an Iraqi truck carried explosives into the United Nations headquarters in Baghdad, a site that should have been treated as untouchable by both sides.

Dunlap's article, which so accurately predicted the coming era of neo-absolutist enemies, did *not* recommend that the United States reciprocate by itself succumbing to neo-absolutism. Precisely to the contrary, it urged that the U.S. military begin to prepare for asymmetric warfare (of the kind the country would experience three years later on 9/11) so that it could maintain an unswerving conformity to international law while defeating its neo-absolutist opponent. Using the long-standing idiom of "chivalry"—a technical term by which international and military law pay tribute to an overarching framework of civil law that endures even in the midst of war—the article insisted that the United States must continue to be Sir Galahad even when confronted by Genghis Khan.

But has the United States continued to uphold the international prohibitions against treachery and other prohibitions against comparable acts of wrongdoing since 9/11? Or has it, without blinking, crossed over into the region of neo-absolutism? Often applied to monarchs and tyrants, the term "absolutism" has, over the last four centuries, been used in the political context to indicate an executive power that is unconstrained by rules or limits.

The gravest evidence against the United States resides in the now elaborately documented acts of torture at Abu Ghraib and the less fully documented instances at interrogation centers in Bagram, Afghanistan (where one prisoner died of pulmonary embolism, another of a heart attack); in Al-Qai'm, Iraq (where an Iraqi general, who voluntarily entered a military camp to inquire about his four sons, died after interrogators beat him, put him head first into a sleeping bag, and sat on his chest); on the British island of Diego Garcia; and at Guantánamo. We also know that the United States has repeatedly sent prisoners to interrogation centers with histories of torture in Syria, Saudi Arabia, Jordan, and Egypt.[2]

The willingness of the United States to torture might well absorb our full attention here. But because it is also the form of neo-absolutism about which most people are already acutely aware, I will only briefly review what we know about it.

In its 2005 annual report, Amnesty International called on national bodies to arrange for "a full and independent investigation" of the "use of torture . . . by U.S. officials" and called for the support of the

International Criminal Court. Determining the degree of responsibility of government leaders for the events at Abu Ghraib must await such an inquiry; but it is important to recognize what the documentary evidence already makes clear: a stark line of influence from Washington to Guantánamo to Bagram to Abu Ghraib.

We know, first, that President Bush and Secretary of Defense Rumsfeld declared that detainees in Guantánamo were not lawful combatants and therefore not protected by international rules governing prisoners of war.[3]

Second, we know that President Bush announced that he *personally* had the power to suspend the Geneva Conventions in Afghanistan. A February 7, 2002, memo from the president to the vice president, secretary of state, secretary of defense, attorney general, CIA director, and chairman of the joint chiefs of staff (among others) stated: "I have the authority under the Constitution to suspend Geneva as between the United States and Afghanistan, but I decline to exercise that authority at this time. . . . I reserve the right to exercise this authority in this or future conflicts."[4]

Third, we know that in Iraq, at Abu Ghraib, individual soldiers—men and women from the 800th Military Police Brigade and the 205th Military Intelligence Brigade—took it upon themselves to suspend Geneva rules and torture detainees. The investigative reports of their acts—the Taguba, Fay-Jones, and Schlesinger Reports—take note of the fact that military-intelligence soldiers who had served in Guantánamo and Bagram later served in Abu Ghraib, carrying with them information about the suspendability of the Geneva Conventions. Key practices at Abu Ghraib—stripping prisoners naked and threatening them with attack dogs—coincide with practices explicitly authorized by Rumsfeld for Guantánamo detainees in a December 2002 memorandum.

The act of torture is such an extreme trespass against the laws of war that it may seem beside the point to wonder whether any other forms of wrong-doing have been carried out; additional acts cannot make a country that tortures worse than it already is, nor would the absence of additional acts diminish its culpability. Yet it is important to consider these others, and in particular perfidy and treachery, because every act that carries us into neo-absolutist territory blurs our vision, makes the boundary easier to cross, and puts us at ever-accelerating risk of carrying out moral harms (such as the use of nuclear weapons) from which we may not soon recover.

International law and military law identify only a tiny set of actions as treachery; it appears that we have committed—or have come perilously close to committing—each of them. Along with torture, the conduct described below reveals a pattern of indifference to even the most elementary moral and legal norms and a willingness to substitute the unbound dictates of men for the rule of law. A good case can be made that the United States has already violated these norms. But even if there have not been criminal violations, there is a pattern in the conduct I consider here, and that pattern suggests a pervasive unwillingness to take the most fundamental norms seriously as strictures that must not be violated. That indifference and that unwillingness are bound, sooner or later, to carry the country into fatal moral terrain.

Rule 1: White Flag, Red Cross

The misuse of a white flag or red cross is considered an act of perfidy. Perfidy is, at its heart, a misuse of signs or pieces of language, according to *International Law—The Conduct of Armed Conflict and Air Operations*, a 1976 pamphlet that is the Air Force's handbook on the laws of warfare. Yet most of the acceptable stratagems of deceit in warfare also involve an intentional misuse or falsification of language. Article 24 of the Hague Conventions, quoted in the Air Force pamphlet, Section 8-4, lists many legitimate falsifications of language: it is lawful to "use enemy signals and passwords" and to issue "bogus orders by an enemy commander"; one may "simulate quiet and inactivity" when a large force is gathering or, conversely, "simulate a large force" when only a small force is present. The list of permissible deceptions is vast. Fraud, as Machiavelli long ago realized, is the natural companion of force.

But the fraudulent use of a white flag or a red cross (or the equivalent of the red cross in other cultures—the red crescent or the red lion, for example) is prohibited for three reasons. First, some small pieces of language in war must remain wholly intact, uncompromised, unwavering, undiluted in their meaning. These few insignia are placed *hors de combat*, or "out of combat"; they constitute a civil structure that remains in place in the international sphere (in the same way that inside a country the military is kept inside a civil frame). These small but sacrosanct pieces of language act as a location from which other true sentences can be spoken: without them, as Morris Greenspan observes in *Modern Law of Land Warfare*, neither party would "be able to place the slightest credence in the word of the other."

The second reason points to the future rather than the present, the period of peace rather than war. Unless certain pieces of language remain uncontaminated by war, no international framework of trust remains available for a truce or peace accord. These small pieces of language must be kept intact because they provide a bridge back to civilization.

The first and second reasons tell us that some pieces of language must carry the guarantee of truthfulness without telling us why *these particular* pieces of language must do so. This explanation is provided by a third principle, which is hard to formulate. One formulation states that no language can be used that "causes the enemy to refrain from violence he would otherwise surely exercise"; another formulation states that it is a "grave breach . . . when the use invites the confidence of the enemy with the intent to betray confidence." These descriptions are both incomplete because acceptable fraud, such as pretending that one's army is not present by moving quietly forward, is intended to "cause the enemy to refrain from violence he would otherwise surely exercise" and also "invites the confidence of the enemy with the intent to betray confidence." What is key in cases of *treachery* is that one party invites its opponents to refrain from injuring others and to refrain from protecting themselves against injury by appealing to the higher frame of language, the hors de combat language, and then, thanks to the opponents' willingness to honor this higher call, injures them. The Iraqi taxi driver who lured the American soldiers toward him asked them to step away from the ground of combat, to stand with him above the battle, but did so only to maneuver the soldiers into harm's way.

So severe is the rule protecting the signs of truce and medical care that it cannot be suspended even for the sake of escape, a circumstance that often permits a relaxation of the rules. For example, it is permissible, for the purpose of escape, to take off one's uniform and wear civilian clothes, an act impermissible in any other combat context.[5] In contrast, it is never permissible for uninjured soldiers to travel in an ambulance, whether they are moving forward into battle or trying to escape.

The stark prohibition on the false use of the red cross is derived from a logically prior and overarching prohibition: that a Red Cross vehicle or building cannot itself be the target of assault. It is because all participants are obligated to regard the white flag and red cross as inviolable that a secondary obligation arises not to use either sign falsely. As the Air Force manual observes, "The rule prohibiting feigning hors de combat status, such as sickness, distress or death, in order to commit or resume hostilities is only a corollary rule to the principle prohibiting attacks on persons who are hors de combat."

What, then, are we to make of the joint Army-Navy-Air Force mission to storm al Nasiriyah General Hospital to take back the injured prisoner of war Private Jessica Lynch? The people of the United States were asked by their government to bear collective witness to this mission—to take it, and honor it, as our national war story. If the narrative captivated national attention, it did so in part because the deeds were so fresh, so unheard of—but they were fresh and unheard of because such deeds are not ordinarily performed, and they are not ordinarily performed because to storm a hospital is to be guilty of perfidy: it is a violation of the primary and overarching prohibition from which the perfidy prohibition is derived.

Did anyone present at the planning session for this mission have a handbook of military rules available? Did anyone object to the plan?[6] For U.S. Special Forces to drive up to the hospital in Nasiriyah in a fleet of ambulances would of course have been a clear act of perfidy. So, too, was it an act of perfidy to arrive at the threshold of the hospital in a fleet of military tanks and helicopters loaded with Navy Seals, Army Rangers, and Air Force pilots, who spilled through the corridors at midnight, breaking down doors and blasting guns. Upon hearing the roar of approaching machinery, the hospital staff, according to their reports, fled to the basement. Inciting members of a medical staff to abandon their posts beside their patients for several hours is a concrete harm, though if they had not abandoned their posts, the United States might now have the slaying of medical personnel and hospital administrators on its hands.

The Navy handbook on the law of naval warfare includes this specific prohibition: "Medical establishments and units, fixed or mobile, and vehicles of wounded and sick or of medical equipment may not be bombarded or attacked." Of the estimated 3,000 Nasiriyan civilians who by that point in the war had been hurt by U.S. armaments, 60 suffering from severed limbs and other severe injuries were housed in the hospital. Private Lynch was transferred to this civilian hospital from a military hospital by her Iraqi captors. Among many untrue elements included in the original dissemination of the story was the image of Iraqi soldiers hovering over Lynch, slapping her to extract information.[7] Both Lynch and the physicians and nurses who cared for her deny that any such incident took place. The inclusion of these false details suggests that the people presenting the story to the American public understood that there is a stringent norm against attacking a hospital and therefore tried to convert the building into something other than a hospital and those hovering near her into brutal interrogators rather than nurses and physicians.

A basic principle governing hospitals in a time of war is *hostes dum vulnerati, fratres*, or "enemies while wounded are brothers," which is generally interpreted to mean that care of injured military forces must be carried out without regard to nationality.[8] This principle was honored at al Nasiriyah General Hospital, where, according to Private Lynch, one of her nurses soothed her body with talc while singing her lullabies. Of her main nurse, Lynch said, "I loved her." Lynch credits her caretakers with giving her life: "I'm so thankful to those people, 'cause that's why I'm alive today," she told Diane Sawyer in a television interview. I am not suggesting that the medical treatment was in any way remarkable. Though some nurses or doctors may have done more than is necessary, decent medical treatment is required both by the Geneva Conventions and by the Red Cross's proposals for regulations on the "safeguard of an enemy hors de combat": "It is forbidden to kill, injure, ill treat or torture an adversary hors de combat. An adversary hors de combat is one who, having laid down his arms, no longer has any means of defense or has surrendered."

The fact that Private Lynch was receiving humane treatment in a hospital does not mean that her broken legs, arm, and spine could be as successfully mended in Iraq as they might be in an American or European hospital. The rules of war allow an injured enemy soldier to be transferred to medical care among her own countrymen, so long as the transfer can be safely made. The day before the U.S. Special Forces raided the hospital, the Iraqi medical staff—as physicians told the BBC and as Private Lynch told ABC—attempted to transport her to an American hospital; but the ambulance was fired on by American soldiers at a checkpoint and forced to turn around. An assault on an ambulance, like an assault on a hospital, is prohibited by national and international regulations. The U.S. soldiers might have thought that the ambulance was a ruse, though the public record does not document the misuse of ambulances by Iraqi forces in Nasiriyah.[9] At best, these actions can be interpreted as answering illegal acts with illegal acts; at worst, they represent the first step in the descent into neo-absolutism.

Some American newspapers called the episode a story of "smoke and mirrors," and, to their credit, the media soon collectively sorted through the story, correcting false information (that Private Lynch had gunshot and stab wounds, rather than broken bones from the truck accident during the ambush; that she stood her ground, killing Iraqis and firing until the moment she was taken, rather than, as she describes, putting down her head and her malfunctioning gun and praying). The creation of an accurate record is the work of many people; it has depended most critically on Private Lynch herself, who demonstrates, among many other forms of valor, an unswerving commitment to the truth.

But what have often seemed to be at issue in these continual corrections are distracting questions about forms and degrees of heroism, whether on the part of Private Lynch, or the Special Forces (who, though their mission was filmed as it took place, are prohibited from speaking about it), or the Nasiriyah medical staff. This constant readjustment of details has obscured a basic question: is it now American practice to conduct raids on hospitals? If Fedayeen soldiers stormed an American hospital in the middle of the night wearing blazing searchlights on their helmets, would we consider that action legal? Admirable? If al Jazeera dedicated several weeks to calibrating the exact level of heroism in the raid, would we believe that the Arab media and their audience were asking the right questions? Are U.S. hospitals, Iraqi hospitals, and International Red Cross facilities on the battlefield now acceptable targets?

ELAINE SCARRY   75

Defenders of the American assault on the hospital might say that it was a legitimate rescue operation. They might say that the hospital was not itself the intended target; it only happened to be where Private Lynch was. The American forces had no choice about the location of the rescue, and the attack was therefore neither against the law nor demonstrative of an indifference to fundamental standards of law and morality.

This interpretation, however flattering to our self-understanding, is hard to reconcile with the facts. The Iraqis were willing to transfer Private Lynch: they were prevented from doing so by the American attack on the ambulance. Moreover, the American government never expressed any regret about the "need" to attack a hospital in service of a rescue operation: instead, the attack was mythologized and celebrated. A lawyer defending the American mission in a war-crimes trial might win his case. But for American citizens who believe that their country should respect fundamental standards, the assault—and the surrounding attitudes—must be deeply troubling. Even if the American assault did not technically violate these standards, it showed no respect for them.

During the first year of the war, we had the numbers and names of U.S. soldiers killed in Iraq, but almost no other information about what was happening on the ground. We did not know at that point even the numbers of Iraqi soldiers and civilians killed and injured, let alone the circumstances of the casualties. In the midst of this heart-sickening vacuum, we were given one story, a story that, properly understood, reveals our own trespass into—or, at a minimum, perilous proximity to—neo-absolutism.

Rule 2: Flying a False Flag

If a country flies a flag that is not its own, the country whose flag it is will surely take offense. The United States has declared it unlawful for a foreign vessel to fly the U.S. flag, and it exacts sanctions against any ship that violates this rule, denying it entry into U.S. ports for three months. During a period of warfare, a neutral country has a special interest in ensuring that its flag not be flown by one of the belligerents, since its use would falsely signal the country's participation on one side or the other, thus making its population vulnerable to reprisal.[10]

But the rules against flying a false flag are not just left up to the special interests and vulnerabilities of particular countries. Chapter 8 of the Air Force pamphlet is dedicated to "Perfidy and Ruses." This chapter includes not only the category of falsified medical and truce signs ("The Misuse of Specified Signs, Signals, and Emblems which are Internationally Recognized") but also a second category: "Misuse of Enemy Flags, Insignia, and Uniform." Hague regulation 23(f)—the basis of the military prohibition—places the false flag in the same category as the misuse of the red cross and white flag: "It is especially prohibited to make improper use of a flag of truce, or the national flag, or of military insignias and uniform of the enemy, as well as of the distinctive signs of the Geneva Convention." Once more, these prohibited falsifications are exceptional cases: almost all words and signs *can* legally undergo mystification during warfare; enemy flags and uniforms reside in that narrow region of language that cannot be misused without making the user guilty of perfidy.

Before the Abu Ghraib revelations, extended *Washington Post* and *New York Times* reports on the alleged American practice of torture in the previous two years indicated that prisoners had been interrogated in rooms where false flags and false national insignia were displayed. Gerald Posner's *Why America Slept* includes a long description of the U.S. torture of alleged al Qaeda terrorist Abu Zubayda. Posner reports the elaborate procedure American interrogators used to disguise themselves and their interrogation room as Saudi Arabian, with the result that the prisoner, believing that he was being questioned by Saudis, revealed his close working relationship with an array of Saudi officials.[11] The CIA (according to Posner) refers to this genre of torture as false-flag interrogation.

Defenders of the event might say that although the Americans were surely flying a false flag, they were not necessarily flying the enemy's flag, or, more precisely, that it was only during the torture session that they learned that the flag they were flying may have belonged to an enemy. Defenders might also say that although many legal analysts before World War II endorsed a blanket prohibition on the use of an enemy flag, since World War II the misuse of the flag is prohibited only during combat.[12] Since torture takes place in a legal vacuum, it cannot be said to exist in the space of combat or the space of non-combat. Therefore, none of the Geneva, Hague, or military rules about uniforms, flags, and insignia apply.

These two arguments are obviously invalid. The stark illegality of torture does indeed place it in a space of moral reprehensibility outside the legal categories of "combat" and "non-combat." But only the most abject cynic would claim that the zone of the morally reprehensible becomes, by virtue of its illegality, a free zone that is exempt from all other rules and laws. Furthermore, the Bush administration has repeatedly insisted that in a war on terrorism, the battlefield is everywhere: a country that unabashedly designated O'Hare International Airport in Chicago a "battlefield" when José Padilla was arrested cannot reasonably hold that a torture room is not a combat zone and therefore not subject to battlefield rules about false flags.

As the battlefield in the war on terrorism is simultaneously everywhere and nowhere, so our enemies are everyone and no one. If the flag we flew in the Zubayda torture room—the flag of Saudi Arabia—was not an enemy flag, it is because we have no enemy. Fifteen of the eighteen hijackers on 9/11 were from Saudi Arabia, so it is hard to see what country would stand ahead in the line of candidates for the designation of "enemy." Are we to suppose that when the Saudi flag is introduced into an interrogation, it has been placed there as the insignia of an American ally or neutral nation and not that of an opponent or suspected opponent? Is it not placed there because our enemy captive may well perceive it (as Zubayda did) as "friendly"?

The Bush administration has treated 9/11 as a shell game of shifting laws and norms. It could have treated the 9/11 attacks as criminal acts and gone after the perpetrators with criminal laws.[13] Instead it has treated them as acts of war and used a framework of war whose battlefields and enemies are everywhere but whose agents are non-state actors and therefore not eligible for Geneva and Hague protections. If our opponents are non-state actors, criminal law, not a deformed version of the laws of war, should hold sway. But shuffling back and forth between two frameworks allows the administration to eliminate all national and international constraints on its increasingly debased power.

The case of Abu Zubayda should not be left behind without pointing out that his treatment violated another elementary rule, beyond the false-flag principle: the requirement that the wounded be treated humanely.

Section 215 of the Army's manual on the law of land warfare describes the "Protection and Care" due the "Wounded and Sick":

> They shall be treated humanely and cared for by the Party to the conflict in whose power they may be, without any adverse distinction founded on sex, race, nationality, religion, political opinions. . . . Any attempts upon their lives, or violence to their persons, shall be strictly prohibited; in particular, they shall not be . . . subjected to torture . . . they shall not be wilfully left without medical assistance and care.

Whether the man being tortured actually was Zubayda, at the time was uncertain (the man refused to say who he was), and whether Zubayda in turn was, as U.S. officials believed, a high-ranking al Qaeda member was also uncertain (he had not stood trial). What was certain was that the man captured had a gunshot wound and was by virtue of his capture hors de combat. He therefore should have been subject to *hostes dum vulnerati, fratres* and should have been cared for without regard to his nationality. Yet Zubayda was denied medical attention until he agreed to cooperate.

In September 2006 the U.S. Army issued a new handbook on interrogation entitled *Human Intelligence Collector Operations*. On page after page it forbids torture (invoking international, national, and military law), but it permits questioning that is free of force, even questioning of a captive who is wounded, so long as the "questioning will not delay the administration of medication to reduce pain" or in any other way jeopardize the captive's medical well-being. In two separate sections it states the prohibition that was violated in the case of Zubayda: "Nor can [the questioner] state, imply, or otherwise give the impression that any type of medical treatment is conditional on the detainee's cooperation in answering questions."

Torture rooms and hospital rooms have come to be blurred in America's wars in Afghanistan and Iraq.

Private Lynch was—by her own account and by the accounts of Nasiriyan physicians, nurses, and hospital administrators—treated in accordance with Section 215 of the Army manual. She was not, as Americans were at first permitted to believed, placed in a medical torture room. But the man called Zubayda, suffering from a gunshot wound in the groin, was placed not in a hospital but in a torture room, and his wound was enlisted into the method of extracting information.

A country at war must identify itself by flags, uniforms, and insignia on its planes. A country at war may not during combat fly a false flag. The United States may not fly the flag of Iraq or Saudi Arabia or Afghanistan or Pakistan. But may it continue to fly the flag of the United States? Can a country that breaks international and national rules—the Hague Conventions, the Geneva Conventions, and the regulations of its own Army, Navy, and Air Force—any longer fly its own flag without being in danger of doing so falsely? The United States that most of us are committed to does not torture, does not conduct raids on the enemy's hospitals, does not shoot at ambulances, does not withhold painkiller from a wounded enemy. Why should the small team of people carrying out such acts be permitted to continue flying our flag?

Rule 3: Wanted, Dead or Alive

On December 14, 2003, Paul Bremer, the American head of the Coalition Provisional Authority (wearing a large tie colored like an American flag, with navy blue at the throat and flaring out into wide red and white stripes), stepped up to the microphone and, referring to the capture of Saddam Hussein, announced, "Ladies and gentlemen, we got him!"

The brief sections on perfidy and treachery in the rules-of-war handbooks of the Air Force, Army, and Navy contain one more regulation, derived from the Hague Conventions, Article 23(b). Here is the way the Air Force pamphlet formulates it:

This article has been construed as prohibiting assassination, proscription or outlawry of an enemy, or putting a price upon an enemy's head, as well as offering a reward for any enemy 'dead or alive.'

The Army handbook, composed earlier, uses similar language to describe the regulation in the section dedicated to "Forbidden Conduct with Respect to Persons." Greenspan's *Modern Law of Land Warfare* explains that these prohibited acts are war crimes:

Under this rule are prohibited acts of assassination, the hiring of assassins, putting a price on an enemy's head, offering a reward for an enemy 'dead or alive,' proscription and outlawry of an enemy . . . . Perpetrators of such acts should be tried as war criminals.

The first formal state prohibition of assassination and the promotion of assassination through the announcement of rewards was issued by President Abraham Lincoln in 1863, as General Order 100:

The law of war does not allow proclaiming either an individual belonging to the hostile army, or a citizen, or a subject of the hostile government, an outlaw, who may be slain without trial by any captor, any more than the modern law of peace allows such international outlawry; on the contrary, it abhors such outrage. The sternest retaliation should follow the murder committed in consequence of such proclamation, made by whatever authority. Civilized nations look with horror upon offers of rewards for the assassination of enemies as relapses into barbarism.

This order influenced the creation of later international prohibitions (which have been incorporated into military law), as well as later American prohibitions in civil law (such as the current Executive Order 12,333).[14]

Against the backdrop of the tripartite prohibition (no assassination, no promise of a reward, no posting of "wanted, dead or alive"), it is useful to review the actions of President Bush. On September 17, 2001, he announced to the country and the world that Osama

bin Laden was "wanted, dead or alive." In his statement, made at a press conference, he referred to this as
a phrase from a Wild West wanted poster, an allusion
that has led at least one worried observer to excuse his
statement as "a figure of speech." Nathan Canestáro,
a member of the CIA's 2001 Afghanistan Task Force,
wrote, "Bush's own suggestion that bin Laden was
'wanted, dead or alive,' strays dangerously close to . . .
prohibited means of killing. Were the statement more
than a figure of speech, it would constitute outlawry,
rendering any resulting deaths as assassination under
international law." But a call to treachery is not dimin-
ished by folksy phrasing.[15] Nor does Canestáro appear
to have reason (other than the wish to make Bush immune to the allegation of grave wrongdoing) to believe
that the announcement was anything but literal.[16]

Soon, as if to reinforce the president's words, an
official reward of $25 million was offered for bin
Laden. A later State Department clarification stressed
that the reward was for information leading to bin
Laden's capture rather than for his body, dead or

alive, but the widely distributed wanted and reward posters did not always include that distinction. An article by Dayna Kaufman in *Fordham Law Review* catalogues the ongoing forms of posting:

> The reward for bin Laden's capture is broadcast for 135 minutes a day in Afghanistan over the Voice of America radio system in Afghanistan's two main languages, Pashto and Dari. The length of the broadcast was expanded by thirty minutes to include daily crime alerts that promote the reward offer exclusively. In addition, the faces and other identifying characteristics of the wanted men [bin Laden and his inner circle] were placed on posters, matchbooks, fliers, and newspaper ads distributed around the world and dropped from United States military planes in Afghanistan.

Once more, the legal issues are arguably complicated, this time by questions about bin Laden's status. Because bin Laden is not a combatant, the laws of war may not apply to him. Here again we see the shell game between criminal law and the laws of war.

If bin Laden is a non-state actor, if he is not a law-ful combatant, he should be sought using criminal law.[17] Instead he is pursued as a war enemy, but the United States is exempt from following the laws of war because the enemy is not a combatant.

Of course, wanted and reward signs have been posted even when the opponent has unquestionably been a state actor. When President Bush's attention pivoted from Afghanistan to Iraq, so did his posters. Perhaps in an attempt to sustain the Wild West sa-loon model, the U.S. military created a deck of cards naming and picturing the 55 most-wanted men in Iraq. Unmindful of the Air Force and Army regu-lations that forbid "putting a price on an enemy's head, offering a reward," the Bush administration offered, and paid, $15 million each for Uday and Qusay Hussein, the sons of Saddam Hussein, and $25 million for their father. A reward of $10 mil-lion was offered for Saddam Hussein's Baath Party deputy, Ibrahim Izzat al Douri. The reward for Abu Musaab al Zarqawi was initially set at $5 million, later raised to $10 million, and still later to $25 million. Lesser amounts have been placed on the heads of other Iraqis. Speaking at a Coalition Provisional Authority briefing, Brigadier General Mark Kimmitt said that the United States put "specific amounts on specific people," though the amounts also depend on whether they are national ($1 million), regional ($200,000), or local ($50,000) terrorists.[18]

I have focused here only on the second and third elements of the tripartite ban (on assassination, on rewards, and on posting wanted signs) because the phrasing of those two bans is relatively uncontroversial, and the Bush administration's violation of—or straying near to violation of—the two bans is also relatively straightforward. Strong disagreements, in contrast, surround the question of what, precisely, national and international law prohibit in the sphere of assassination, and such disagreements therefore also make it difficult to determine how close the Bush administration has come to assassination (in the killing of Uday and Qusay Hussein) or to attempted assassination (on the night before the opening of war in Iraq, when the United States repeatedly bombed a house where Saddam Hussein was believed to be staying). All sources agree that if a commander in chief or national leader or public figure participates in a battle and is killed in that battle (either intentionally or unintentionally), no act of assassination has occurred. If, however, one side goes behind the line of combat and intentionally kills a political leader on the other side, that act is widely understood to be an act of assassination.

But on this not everyone agrees. Several military analysts argue that the assassination of enemy leaders is legal under international law, that it is not in and of itself treacherous and only becomes so if treacherously carried out. This view is expressed by W. Hays Parks (writing in 1989 in *Army Lawyer*), by Air Force Major Michael N. Schmitt (writing in 1992 in the *Yale Journal of International Law*), and by Major Tyler J. Harder (writing in 2002 in *Military Law Review*).[19] Although these men are military analysts, their interpretations appears to deviate from the Air Force and Army handbooks' summaries of Hague regulation 23(b) by inverting the categories. These handbooks list assassination as a prohibited act of treachery (along with reward postings and "wanted, dead or alive" announcements). In other words, assassination is a subcategory of treachery. The two handbooks do not (as we might imagine from reading the cited articles) have a section on assassination that is subdivided into legal forms and illegal, treacherous forms. Parks, Schmitt, and Harder do not believe that there are acceptable and unacceptable "wanted, dead or alive" signs or acceptable and unacceptable "reward" postings, so it is odd that the third prohibited act, which occupies the same grammatical position in the sentence as the other two, is imagined in this way.

A second indication that this dissenting view is mistaken comes from the logical incoherence that it introduces into the relations between the three parts of the tripartite division. A treacherous assassination, in this view, involves "surprise"; it involves harm to someone who has reason to believe you wish him no injury (such as someone who agreed to meet you to discuss an armistice). Harder, arguing that only violations of confidence make assassination illegal, states, "Treachery is a breach of confidence or perfidious act, that is, an attack on an individual who justifiably believes he has nothing to fear from the attacker."[20] But this view is starkly incompatible with the other two parts of the ban—the prohibition on wanted signs and rewards. What could be more open and unsurprising than a straightforward announcement that a country intends to have an enemy leader killed? A wanted sign or a reward poster constitutes just such an open announcement. Prohibiting assassination only if it entails a violation of confidence or surprise utterly contradicts the ban on rewards and wanted postings.[21]

Even if one were to take the view offered by Harder, Parks, and Schmitt—that no act of intentionally killing political leaders will be deemed assassination unless it involves a betrayal of confidence—the actions of the United States in Afghanistan and Iraq do not appear to stand entirely in the clear.[22] Once wanted-signs, or their equivalents, have been posted, a political leader will almost certainly go into deep hiding. Who, then, is offered the reward for information leading to that leader's capture? It cannot be offered to random citizens of the country or passersby or taxi drivers or witnesses in the marketplace; it cannot be offered to acquaintances or even to ordinary friends and family members. It is offered only to the one or two closest intimates in whom the leader places so much confidence that he has entrusted them with his hiding.[23]

The person who informed the U.S. military where they would find Uday and Qusay Hussein (and who has since collected the $30 million reward) was Nawaf al Zaidan, in whose house the brothers had been staying for the 22 days before he revealed their location. Lists containing Nawaf al Zaidan's name as well as the names of 48 of his relatives were later posted by Iraqis on the walls of Mosul as targeted for death because, as *The Guardian* explained, they were seen as having violated the host-guest relation: "Mr. Zaidan betrayed one of the most closely-held principles of tribal law: that a host has an obligation to protect his guests." While the prohibition on betraying the host-guest bond is indeed a principle of tribal law and may sound ancient to American ears, it must be noted how close it is to the prohibition on treachery in international law, since it involves injuring or killing someone who had reason to place confidence in you. Insofar as rewards and wanted signs are addressed to the hosts in whose care the wanted men have placed themselves, they are addressed to those who—in the eyes of the person in hiding—appear to be holding a white flag. Therefore, even if we accept the Harder, Parks, and Schmitt doctrine that assassination is illegal only if it entails a violation of confidence, the United States may be guilty.

Where Do We Stand?

Our country tortures. It conducts raids on hospitals. It flies false flags. It makes "wanted, dead or alive" pronouncements. It posts rewards. It attempts (and sometimes carries out) assassinations. International law and military law do not put endless restraints on national actors. The sections on perfidy and treachery in the Air Force, Army, and Navy handbooks are in each case extremely brief—they put only three rules in front of us. Yet we have been unable to remain true to the three, or even two of the three, or even one of the three. We have violated, or have come perilously close to violating, each of them.

What judgments would we make if we altered the location and agent of these acts? Were we to look at al Qaeda's literature and find there "wanted, dead or alive" postings for Western leaders or Western citizens, would we not regard those papers as documentary proof of neo-absolutism—proof of a complete disregard for international and military law? If a Saudi billionaire offered $30 million to any American who could identify a place in which an American leader or ordinary citizen could be captured or killed, what would we think? Would we say that the offer stays safely in the realm of legal practice because no one's confidence has been betrayed? Or because the offer only asked for information leading to capture? Would we say that it was just a figure of speech, an imitation of American rhetoric? If our opponents shot at our ambulances or if they raided our hospitals to retrieve their injured soldiers, what would we think?

Article 503 of the Army manual, directly following a passage describing acts the Geneva Conventions deem "grave breaches," quotes the Conventions: "No High Contracting Party"—that is, a signatory nation—"shall be allowed to absolve itself or any other High Contracting Party of any liability incurred by itself or by another High Contracting Party in respect of breaches referred to in the preceding Article." How, then, have we come to absolve ourselves of these breaches, or perhaps more to the point, how have we come to believe that no absolution is needed?

From the outset, the U.S. government's recognition that it might be guilty of wrongdoing has been visible in attempts not to right its conduct but to rewrite the rules. The correspondence between the White House and the Office of Legal Counsel during the winter of 2002—specifically Alberto Gonzales's January 25 memorandum and John Ashcroft's February 1 letter, both addressed to President Bush—shows an administration making legal decisions with the goal of making U.S. officials immune to conviction of war crimes. Gonzales advises Bush: "[Adhere] to your determination that [Geneva Convention III on the Treatment of Prisoners of War] does not apply" since that will "guard effectively against . . . misconstruction or misapplication of Section 2441 [the War Crimes Act]." Ashcroft writes: "A determination that the Geneva Convention does not apply will provide the United States with the highest level of legal certainty" so that our actions will be "foreclosed from judicial review."

The most effective way to make oneself immune to the charge of war crimes is to abstain from committing war crimes. Our alternative procedure might be called "cubing the violation": violate the rule in practice by carrying out actual harms to human beings, violate the rule in theory by deforming or revising the rule itself, violate the rule in metapractice by taking away from the courts the right to review the violations at levels one and two. The threefold injury to persons, rules, and courts has extended well beyond the legal memos of 2002. President Bush later attempted to write into a new detainee-treatment bill a provision granting immunity to war-crime charges for its CIA counterterrorism officers, a provision Congress rejected. The CIA counterterrorism officers themselves are, according to *The Washington Post* and *The New York Times*, buying insurance policies in record numbers that will help cover their court costs should they eventually be tried for their acts during this period. The new detainee-treatment bill, called the Military Commissions Act and signed into law on October 17, 2006, permits the executive branch to rewrite the habeas corpus rule, thereby delivering a huge blow to persons and courts. The Act eliminates from our courts the right to review executive-branch decisions about detainees by prohibiting prisoners from challenging their detention in court.

Often during the past five years it has been the military that has made the best—if ultimately unsuccessful—effort to protect our framework of national and international law. It was Colin Powell who held out the longest against administration pressure to give false evidence of Iraqi nuclear weapons; it was Specialist Joseph Darby who made the Abu Ghraib photographs available to the world; it was the judge advocates general who continually protested detainee treatment in Guantánamo until the Supreme Court could act; it was Senator John McCain, explicitly on the basis of military experience, who repeatedly repelled President Bush's attempts to legalize torture.

But this resistance is imperfect and cannot always hold out, as became clear in Powell's eventual UN testimony on Iraq's nuclear weapons and in McCain's eventual endorsement of the devastating Military Commissions Act. The new Army handbook on interrogation is a third case in point: it frequently reiterates the prohibition on torture and brainwashing, even explicitly listing and forbidding the elements (dogs, nakedness, hoods) that were designated permissible in Secretary Rumsfeld's December 2002 memorandum on detainee treatment in Guantánamo. But one practice that Rumsfeld permitted in his April 2003 memorandum to the Southern Command—the false-flag interrogation—has made its way into the handbook as an acceptable practice, as have other practices that should not be there.[24]

And what if the military does manage to hold the line? What if over time we come to see again and again that our civilian leaders do not obey the law and our military leaders do? And that our civilian leaders do not know how to safeguard the American population and our military leaders do? (Hurricane Katrina is an example: only when the military arrived did rescue begin.) Would this lead to our eventually preferring military over civilian leadership? It is exactly this situation that Charles Dunlap—the writer with whom we began—warns against in an earlier, 1992 article entitled "The Origins of the American Military Coup of 2012," an article that ought to be as widely read and debated in the civilian world as it has been in the military world.

But let us return to the immediate problem of neo-absolutism. To our earlier question—how have we come to believe that no acknowledgment of wrongdoing is needed?—three others can be added.

First, we know that our terrorist opponents resort to treachery because they cannot match our military force; they must choose between accepting defeat at the outset or else opposing us through asymmetric warfare. But given our own military prowess, why do we resort to treachery?

Second, if the counterpart to treachery in the realm of weapons is unconventional weapons, why should we believe that our current leaders, willing to countenance torture and treachery, will refrain from using unconventional weapons? Though Iraq has no nuclear weapons, the United States has thousands. If our leaders are willing to perform actions prohibited by our own military manuals, what will restrain them from performing actions that our military manuals assure us are legal? A version of the following sentence appears in the Air Force, Army, and Navy handbooks on the laws of war:

> There is at present no rule of international law expressly prohibiting States from the use of nuclear weapons in warfare. In the absence of express prohibition, the use of such weapons against enemy combatants and other military objectives is permitted.[25]

Third, even if we successfully refrain from neo-absolutist practices, and even if those who oppose us eventually agree to give them up, is the situation that brought neo-absolutism into being at all tolerable? Is it tolerable that one country should have such uncontested military might that it can force every other country on earth to accept the boundaries that are now in place, the moral definitions that are now in place, the distribution of goods that is now in place? It is hard to imagine a conception of political fairness that could endorse so brutal an asymmetry.

Most of the peace plans that have ever been written have included a provision that allows countries, after trying to settle disagreements peacefully, to go to war. Without this possibility, the world remains frozen in place in a way that arbitrarily advantages countries that at a single point in time became most powerful. The sphere in which this question continues to be most important is that of nuclear weapons—their steady proliferation abroad and their vast and terrifying numbers on our own submarines and our own ground.

3

Presidential Crimes
(September 2008)

WE HAVE AT PRESENT TWO GOVERNMENT LEADERS, a president and a vice president, who, according to all available evidence, have carried out grave crimes. Will these two men leave office and live out their lives without being subjected to legal proceedings? Such proceedings will surely release new documents and provide additional testimony important in resolving their guilt or innocence. But the public record is now so elaborate, so detailed, and validated from so many directions that a weight is on the population's shoulders: does our *already existing knowledge* of what they have done obligate us to press for legal redress?

The question is painful even to ask, so painful that we may all yield to an easy temptation not to pursue it at all.

A major seduction away from prosecution is the euphoria that has surrounded the 2008 election campaign, even as the contest sharpens. "America at its Best" reads the front cover of the June 5, 2008 issue of *The Economist*, with a photograph of Barack Obama and John McCain pictured there. The elated sense that we might be restored to dignity in our own eyes and in the eyes of the world has rightly been credited first and foremost to Obama, to his spiritual carriage, his open cadences, his refusal to degrade opponents or adversaries. But McCain, too, is responsible for the atmosphere of well-being. Despite the large areas of overlap between his beliefs and those of George Bush, he has come before the electorate with a voice free of greed and cruelty. On countless occasions, he has spoken clearly about torture at a time when many other people have spoken confusedly.

This confidence in the power of the presidential nominees to restore us to ourselves is based above all on one attribute—not charisma, not eloquence, not heroism, but another quality that they share: their commitment to the rule of law. Since November will almost surely bring a return to the rule of law, why not devote our energies and full attention to the electoral process? To keep our eyes on the nominees is to be filled with renewed self-belief; to turn back to the current administration is to feel heartsick and ashamed. Why willingly look in one direction when one can look in the other?

First, because November will only "almost surely," not surely, bring a return to the rule of law. Between now and November, any one of us could be taken ill, and so could one of the candidates. If John McCain suddenly became ill, for example, the Republican commitment to the rule of law would instantly cease to exist with clarion certainty. Anyone who doubts that a return to confusion is possible should be reminded that as late as this spring—when Bush vetoed a bill that outlawed the use of torture by the CIA—Congress failed to achieve the two-thirds affirmative vote that would override the veto. The vote, like other congressional votes on torture, split along party lines. The pool of candidates committed to the rule of law is not deep: there are no back-up Republican candidates who have spoken out decisively against torture or on behalf of the need to close Guantánamo. Moreover, McCain or Obama might lapse from law. Indeed, McCain—whose aggressive insistence on war with Iraq began within days of 9/11—voted with his party and President Bush on the CIA bill. McCain has consistently opposed making the federal courts available to detainees, and he condemned the recent Supreme Court decision ensuring habeas corpus protections for Guantánamo detainees as "one of the worst" in the country's history.

Still, and this is a second reason to address the wrongdoing of the current administration, let us suppose what is fair to suppose, that Barack Obama and John McCain continue in good health, are as wedded to the law as they appear, that one of the two is elected fairly and honestly, and that the country begins its mighty pivot back to its gravitational center in the rule of law. It will be almost like a miracle cure, an overnight release from our eight-year-long affliction.

Or will it? What will this shift to the rule of law mean? It will mean that when we are led by a person who does *not* believe in the rule of law, we will *not* as a country follow the rule of law; and when we are led by a person who *does* believe in the rule of law, we *will* follow the rule of law. If that is the case, the United States will continue to be what it has been during the last eight years: a country governed by the rule of men (their beliefs, their preferences, their choices), not by the rule of law (where beliefs, preferences, and choices are constrained by invariable and nonnegotiable prohibitions on cruelty and fraud). Just as one might in the past have said, "this president was short whereas the next president was tall" or "this president was isolationist whereas as the next president was internationalist," so now one might shrug and say, "this president believed it was his prerogative to torture whereas the next president believed it was not." The incalculable damage left by Bush and Cheney's day-in-and-day-out contempt for national and international law may sweep forward in time and trivialize into a matter of personal preference any future president's adherence to the law. Will we become a country in which the rule of law is just another policy preference? Do we really think that the rule of law is to be left in the hands of our leaders?

In deciding about legal redress, we need to be clear about the large stakes in our decision. The very multiplicity of the apparent crimes, the sheer array of arguably broken laws, is dizzying. But that multiplicity must be faced, for in it we will see that what got in President Bush's way was not any one law but the rule of law itself. It is the rule of law that has been put in jeopardy by a project of executive domination; it is the rule of law that will continue to be in peril; and it is only, therefore, by addressing the crimes through legal instruments—through a formal, legal arena, and not simply through the electoral repudiation of bad policy—that the grave and widespread damage stands a chance of being repaired.

Applying the Law in Towns, Courts, and Congress

On March 4, 2008, the citizens of Brattleboro, Vermont went to the polls and voted by a count of 2,012 to 1,795 to endorse the recommendation that if President Bush or Vice President Cheney came to that town, they should be "arrested and detained" for "crimes against our Constitution." The citywide vote on Brattleboro's non-binding resolution was the third step in a many-months-long process that scrupulously followed the procedures laid out in a section of the Brattleboro Town Charter entitled "Powers of the People." In winter 2007 a petition (written and circulated by town resident Kurt Daims) was signed by the required 5 percent of the population. Then in January the Board of Selectman, by a three to two vote, forwarded the issue to the town-wide ballot scheduled for early spring.

How likely is it that President Bush or Vice President Cheney will visit Vermont, the single state in the country that George Bush has not entered in his first seven-and-a-half-years in office? Less likely, even, than it was before March 4. This still leaves a large geography in which the pair are at liberty.

Or does it? In the recent history of U.S. cities, one city often acts as the catalyst for hundreds of others: in January 2002, Ann Arbor, Michigan passed a resolution voicing its noncompliance with the Patriot Act; there are now 406 towns (and eight states) that have passed similar resolutions.[1] So, too, the governing councils of 92 towns have, by a formal vote, called upon the U.S. Congress to begin impeachment proceedings against President Bush and Vice President Cheney.[2] Perhaps not surprisingly, thirty-nine of those towns are in Vermont, twenty-one in Massachusetts, but the roll call of states represented includes California, Oregon, Wisconsin, Michigan, Illinois, Colorado, North Carolina, Maryland, Ohio, New Hampshire, and New York.

So far, only one other city has reenacted the Brattleboro arrest resolution. In a town meeting in the spring of 2008, Marlboro, Vermont voted 43 to 25 to draft and publish indictments of the country's president and vice president, and "to arrest and detain" them should they arrive in town. But what if over the coming years the number of towns that formally vote to indict and arrest President Bush and Vice President Cheney steadily grows and eventually—as in the case of the town resolutions in favor of presidential impeachment or the resolutions against the Patriot Act—reaches the number 92 or 402? Cross-country travel will then become more restrictive for the former president and vice president. The felt-duty of the population to uphold the rule of law will be encoded in the geography of the country. These efforts provide a powerful historical record whether or not they result in a forcible assertion of the rule of law.

Can the harm done by Bush and Cheney be addressed through a more direct application of law? Vincent Bugliosi—who has successfully prosecuted twenty-one murder cases (most famously, Charles Manson) and eighty-four other felonies (losing only one case)—argues that Bush's fabrications about Iraq's weapons of mass destruction, connection to al Qaeda, and status as an imminent threat to the United States provide the legal basis for charging him with murder[3] and trying him in any state that meets one condition: that it is the former residence of a soldier who has died in Iraq. All fifty states meet that condition.[4] Bugliosi's *The Prosecution of George W. Bush for Murder* presents the argument for prosecution, and after publication, Bugliosi forwarded a copy of the book to every state's attorney general and offered his assistance to any office that takes on the case.

Some of Bugliosi's early chapters have the lurching rage of a grieving parent. (Most of us have a more anemic form of citizenship and can watch with poise as 4000 twenty-year-olds die believing they are fighting the country that struck us on 9/11.) But the central chapters—on evidence, case law, jurisdiction, court arguments, and the lack of any exonerating defense—

display a dispassionate master prosecutor at work. Convinced that the defendant is guilty of mass murder and conspiracy to commit murder, this citizen means to win this case. Though each of the fifty states provides an appropriate venue, Bugliosi argues that a federal district court (the country has 93) would be an even more appropriate site: Washington, D. C. heads the list. Prosecution can begin at any time after President Bush leaves office (he is immune while in office), and there is no statute of limitations.

As Bugliosi's preference for a federal rather than a state venue suggests, the main domestic arena for addressing the administration's aggressive dismantling of the rule of law is not the individual citizen, town, or state, but the federal government: the Congress and the Supreme Court. The Senate's recently released *Report on Whether Public Statements Regarding Iraq by U.S. Government Officials Were Substantiated by Intelligence Information* points in the same direction. While it does not make a case for murder prosecutions, it is nonetheless a devastating document, meticulous and relentless, that buttresses Bugliosi's argument about culpable deceptions.

The *Senate Report* takes five major policy statements about Iraq between late August 2002 and early February 2003—three speeches by President Bush, one by Vice President Cheney, one by Secretary of State Powell—and juxtaposes the information contained in specific sentences to the information available at the time from the intelligence community. It then draws on an array of other sentences spoken by top officials, including Secretary of Defense Rumsfeld and National Security Advisor Condoleezza Rice, and assesses their accuracy. This same sentence-by-sentence procedure is followed across eight categories: nuclear weapons, biological weapons, chemical weapons, weapons of mass destruction in general, weapons delivery systems, connections to terrorism, regime intent, and forecasts of post-war Iraq.

Two discrepancies are striking: between what the leaders of our country said about Iraq's nuclear weapons and what the intelligence community believed at the time, and between what the leaders of our country said about Iraq's connections to al Qaeda, before and after September 11, and what the intelligence community believed at the time.

The two subjects have a crucial effect on one another in creating the impression that Iraq poses an imminent nuclear threat to the United States. If Iraq has or is close to having a nuclear weapon but has no will to attack us, we remain in a safety zone: many countries have nuclear weapons; some of them, such as the United States, have thousands. If, conversely, Iraq is collaborating with al Qaeda but has no nuclear weapon (or other weapons of mass destruction), we once more remain in relative safety. Only if the two features are simultaneously present do we enter a high-alarm zone.

The two lies together proved to be much more potent than either one alone in building an alternative, extra-legal universe. The escalating use of the commander-in-chief clause to amplify presidential power is magnified once the country is fighting not a metaphorical war (a war on terror) but a literal war against another state, armed with weapons of mass destruction and ready to use them, perhaps by making them available to a proxy.

The virtuoso sentence-by-sentence *Senate Report* shows that the Bush administration starkly lied on the subject of Iraq's collaboration with al Qaeda. The intelligence community repeatedly stated that it could find no reliable evidence of such a partnership: "Intelligence assessments, including multiple CIA reports and the November 2002 National Intelligence Estimate dismissed the claim that Iraq and al Qaeda were cooperating partners."[5] President Bush, in contrast, repeatedly announced that they worked together:

> Al Qaeda hides, Saddam doesn't, but the danger is, is that they work in concert. The danger is, is that al Qaeda becomes an extension of Saddam's madness and his hatred and his capacity to extend weapons of mass destruction around the world. . . . you can't

distinguish between al Qaeda and Saddam when you talk about the war on terror.[6]

The intelligence community noted a single source, Ibn al-Shaykh al-Libi, who spoke of Saddam Hussein providing al Qaeda with biological- and chemical-weapons training. But the intelligence reports on this information always stipulate that the man appears to be a fabricator.[7] Once the war was underway, al-Libi—who had been renditioned to Egypt—acknowledged that he fabricated the information because he was threatened with (and was possibly subjected to) torture; only by giving the information his interrogators appeared to want, he alleges, could he stop the interrogation.[8] According to Powell's chief of staff, Lawrence Wilkerson, this misinformation played a decisive role in Powell's willingness to make his UN speech, though he had no idea the information was elicited under coercion.[9]

The National Intelligence Estimate showed that there was no intelligence indicating Iraq's intention to supply al Qaeda with weapons of mass destruction. But this claim was repeatedly made by President Bush ("Iraq has longstanding ties to terrorist groups which are capable of, and willing to, deliver weapons of mass destruction"), Vice President Cheney ("The war on terror will not be won 'till Iraq is completely and verifiably deprived of weapons of mass destruction"), and others, such as Secretary of State Powell and Deputy Secretary of Defense Paul Wolfowitz.[10] This constant assertion that al Qaeda and Iraq worked hand-in-hand made it possible for President Bush to announce in his March 17, 2003 "Address to the Nation" that "with the help of Iraq, the terrorists could fulfill their stated ambitions and kill thousands or hundreds of thousands of innocent people in our country."[11]

The *Senate Report* shows that on the subject of Iraq's nuclear weapons program President Bush and Vice President Cheney again fabricated, but this time not as starkly. Rather than issuing announcements that had no basis whatsoever in existing intelligence, they revised the intelligence community's picture by exaggeration and omission.

One way to describe Iraq's level of nuclear readiness is on a scale that goes from one, where that country has no program at all for producing nuclear weapons, to four, where it has an actual weapon in hand. Postwar intelligence would eventually certify that Iraq, in the months and years before the war began, was at level one, with no attempt underway to develop nuclear weapons, nor any programs to develop chemical or biological weapons. But prior to the war, the intelligence reports were divided between level one and level two. For example, in the fall of 2002 the State Department's Bureau of Intelligence and Research stated its view that Iraq had no program for reconstituting nuclear weapons; the National Intelligence Estimate, in contrast, stated that one was underway. No divided judgment, however, is registered in White House statements, which instead used adrenalized constructions, such as the following from Dick Cheney: "We now have *irrefutable evidence* that he has . . . set up and reconstituted his program," and "we know he has been *absolutely devoted* to trying to acquire nuclear weapons. And we believe he has, *in fact*, reconstituted nuclear weapons."[12]

Aluminum tubes were at the center of a similar instance of division within the intelligence community that was translated into univocal certainty by the administration. The CIA and the Department of Energy disagreed about whether aluminum tubes procured by Iraq were destined for nuclear weapons or instead the more benign purpose of rocket construction.[13] President Bush and National Security Advisor Rice repeatedly cited the aluminum tubes, and never mentioned the disagreement.[14]

If the intelligence community said "no," the administration said "maybe"; if the intelligence community said "maybe," the administration said "certainly." If the intelligence community said "long time," the administration said "tomorrow." For example, the intelligence community repeatedly stated that even if Saddam Hussein had a weapons program, it would take five to seven years to complete (with a caveat that if Iraq could acquire weapons parts from another country, the final product could be ready in one year). With the exception of Secretary of State Powell's February 2003 speech to the United Nations, the five-to-seven year window is simply never mentioned by anyone in the administration.[15]

The intelligence community assessments on nuclear weapons never strayed beyond level two. The Bush Administration, in contrast, started at level two and slid up toward the highest zone of alarm. Insofar as the Bush administration acknowledged any uncertainty, it repositioned the site of it. Rather than locating the question mark (as the intelligence community had) at the boundary between "no interest in weapons development" and "attempts now underway at developing weapons," the administration shifted the question mark to the line between "having the weapon" and "using the weapon." "The first time we may be completely certain he has a—nuclear weapon is when, God forbids, he uses one," President Bush announced in September of 2002.[16] In the months that followed, Bush would repeatedly sound the alarm: "Facing clear evidence of peril we cannot wait for the final proof—the smoking gun—that could come in the form of a mushroom cloud."[17]

The *Senate Report* contains a critical minority report from some Republican members of the Select Committee on Intelligence that, on close inspection, does nothing to weaken the majority report. For example, the minority report is at pains to show that members of Congress are themselves on record as having echoed the reckless statements about Iraq's nuclear weapons.[18] But far from exonerating President Bush, Vice President Cheney, and Secretary of State Powell, the record of these statements by senators helps us comprehend why having leaders lie about highly classified information is devastating. A president's words have, and should have, *transmissible authority*.[19] It ought to be the case that a member of congress or an everyday citizen hearing the president's statements can rely on the leader's scrupulous accuracy and therefore repeat those words. A president's words—that the country was conceived in liberty, that we have nothing to fear but fear itself, that we should guard against unwarranted influence by the military-industrial complex, that we should ask what we can do for our country—will, through repetition, eventually become part of the population's own words; they will be dispersed throughout the verbal fabric of the country.[20] The office of the presidency is a site of widespread emulation; that is why the act of violating that office by lying to Congress and the country about national security should be regarded as a high crime, thus meeting the Constitution's standard for impeachment and removal. Perhaps the offense should be called not "Lying" but "Lying-While-Holding-an-Office-that-Will-Inspire-Millions-of-Repetitions-of-the-Lies and-Tens-of-Thousands-of-Deaths."

Finally, the majority report, which is almost wholly dedicated to juxtaposing sentences spoken by the administration with sentences issued by the intelligence community, briefly notes two additional avenues of fabrication that the administration followed. First, various sectors of the intelligence community themselves were under White House pressure to come up with suitable answers. The question, then, is not just, did the White House exaggerate minimal information given by intelligence? but did the White House exaggerate minimal information that had itself been produced under pressure from the White House?[21] Second, the White House has the power to declassify intelligence information selectively: President Bush released information that he wanted a wider readership to see and kept other intelligence (that presented an alternative or dissenting view) classified.[22] The *Senate Report* directs attention to, but does not provide a sustained study of, the two problems.[23]

The president and his highest officers together erected a vast structure of lies about Iraq's phantom nuclear partnership with al Qaeda. But is this latticework of lies itself a prosecutable crime? What is the crime? "Murder, conspiracy to commit murder, and aiding and assisting murder," says Vincent Bugliosi, triable in either state or federal court. Others might say that the deceptions leading to war are "crimes against humanity" and "crimes against peace." Still others think that impeachment and removal are the place to start.

On June 10, 2008 Congressmen Dennis Kucinich from Ohio and Robert Wexler from Florida cosponsored 35 articles of impeachment outlining the grounds for indicting George Bush. Included in the list of impeachable offenses are the President's fabrications about Iraq's nuclear weapons; his direct lies about Iraq's connections to al Qaeda; his retaliation against those who tried to tell the truth about the lack of nuclear weapons in Iraq, specifically his felonious disclosure of Valerie Plame Wilson's clandestine CIA identity; his authorization and encouragement of torture as official policy; his direct responsibility for rendition; his illegal detention of "U.S. citizens and foreign captives" (including the "imprisonment of children"); his warrantless wiretapping; his failure to protect the United States by heeding pre-9/11 warnings; his failure to protect soldiers in Iraq with proper armor; his failure to protect the residents of New Orleans in the wake of Hurricane Katrina; his acts instructing subordinates to disregard congressional subpoenas; and his 1,100 signing statements releasing him from carrying out even those laws passed during his own administration. The House voted to forward the articles of impeachment to the Judiciary Committee. The articles of impeachment against George Bush are now side by side in the Judiciary Committee with articles of impeachment against Dick Cheney, first presented to the House of Representatives by Congressman Kucinich in the fall of 2007.

The Crime at the Center

While the grounds of impeachment are appropriately numerous, and lying in the run-up to the Iraq War is one essential ground, it is crucial for the country to recognize that there is one crime with a legal profile so singular that it can—even standing alone—convey the wholesale contempt for the rule of law displayed by the Bush administration. That crime is the act of torture. The absolute prohibition on torture in national and international law, as Jeremy Waldron argued in *Columbia Law Review*, "epitomizes" the "spirit and genius of our law," the prohibition "draw[s] a line between law and savagery," it requires a "respect for human dignity" even when "law is at its most forceful and its subjects at their most vulnerable." The absolute rule against torture is foundational and minimal: it is the bedrock on which the whole structure of law is erected. It is only "our clear grip on [this] well-known prohibition" that acts as a "crucial point of reference for sustaining . . . less confident beliefs" about other prohibitions.[24]

The congressional articles of impeachment include "Authorizing, and Encouraging the Use of Torture." Congress has begun to address the crime along other avenues of action that may remain independent from, or instead contribute to, the impeachment effort. Crucial to these efforts has been the research carried out by British barrister Philippe Sands and published in his 2008 book *Torture Team: Rumsfeld's Memo and the Betrayal of American Values.* Sands's essential point is that the pressure for torture originated in the White House, not—as the White House has tried to portray—among military interrogators at Guantánamo. Top attorneys—Attorney General Alberto Gonzales (then legal counsel for Bush), David Addington (legal counsel for Cheney), and William Haynes (legal counsel for Rumsfeld)—together visited Guantánamo with almost no other discernible purpose than to make clear to the military interrogators there how keenly the White House was awaiting whatever new information they could elicit.[25]

Sands's *Torture Team* is not only a riveting book but a brilliantly designed and executed legal case with a series of witnesses for the prosecution taking the stand and together providing a set of damning revelations. Focused on the 54 consecutive days of torture inflicted on one prisoner, Mohammed al-

Qahtani (against whom all legal charges were eventually dropped), the case, by the very pressure of its single-mindedness, successfully shows that President Bush's team was in direct contact with the room in which the physical injury was taking place. Sands shows not only that White House attorneys personally visited Guantánamo to convey the president, vice president, and secretary of defense's personal interest in "information" produced by the interrogations, but that between January 12 and January 15, 2003, Secretary of Defense Rumsfeld—who was under steady pressure from Navy General Counsel Alberto Mora to rescind the list of fifteen torture techniques that he, Rumsfeld, had personally authorized—was buying time. Rumsfeld hoped that in those additional 72 hours the continuing torture of al-Qahtani would at last yield the hoped-for information before he issued the order that the torture cease.

Did those interrogating al-Qahtani have a direct telephone line into Rumsfeld's office during that last seventy-two hours? During the 1, 296 hours of the full 54 days? That question and others will inevitably be asked during formal legal inquiries into White House torture either in Congress or in a courtroom.

Though focused on one prison and one prisoner, Sands's book sets up an echo chamber in which years of revelations suddenly gather cumulative force. His book obligates us to remember all the instances of direct White House pressure that other investigatory reports have shown. For example, just as attorneys Gonzales, Addington, and Haynes personally visited Guantánamo, so a "senior member of the National Security Council" made a parallel visit to Abu Ghraib in November 2003.

Brigadier General Janis Karpinski described the visit to the authors of the 2004 *Schlesinger Report*, who summarized her words. The visit led "some personnel at the facility to conclude, perhaps incorrectly, that even the White House was interested in the intelligence gleaned from their interrogation reports."[26] In Karpinski's August 3, 2005 interview with Jefferson

Law School professor Marjorie Cohn, Karpinski revealed that posted on a pole at Abu Ghraib was a short list of interrogation techniques (including the use of dogs, stress positions, and withholding of food) signed by Secretary of Defense Rumsfeld with a handwritten postscript, "Make sure this happens!!"[27] Top administration pressure for more "information" has also been described by former Pentagon lawyer Richard Schiffrin. Schiffrin, speaking to *The New York Times* on the eve of his June 2008 testimony before the Senate Armed Services Committee, stated that Rumsfeld's lawyer, Haynes, and others repeatedly "expressed 'great frustration' that the military was not effectively obtaining information from prisoners," and complained that "the intelligence being obtained from detainees" was "insufficient."[28] These reports all indicate that the White House not only suspended the Geneva Conventions and signed the list of torture techniques, but personally leaned on the torturers to get "answers."

In response to a report issued by the Inspector General in the Justice Department describing open debate at the White House about torture techniques, 59 members of Congress have written a letter to the Justice Department urging the appointment of a special counsel to investigate whether President Bush and other high executive officers are guilty of crimes of torture.[29] The Senate Armed Services Committee also requested that Haynes (along with others) testify on the issue of interrogation practices in June 2008.[30] And retired Major General Antonio Taguba, who authored one of the early studies of the abuse carried out by soldiers and military police at Abu Ghraib, has made public his assessment of the part played by the White House inner circle in formulating and promulgating a government policy of torture: "There is no longer any doubt as to whether the current administration has committed war crimes. The only question that remains to be answered is whether those who ordered the use of torture will be held to account."[31]

Some hope for legal redress of the kind that Taguba calls for comes from the willingness of courts to resist presidential authority, as the very names of the leading Supreme Court cases indicate: *Rasul v. Bush, Hamdan v. Rumsfeld, Boumediene v. Bush.*

In *Rasul v. Bush* the court ruled six to three that detainees held at Guantánamo can challenge the legality of their detention in U.S. courts. Writing for the majority, Justice Stevens stressed that historically the writ of habeas corpus is, at its core, "a means of reviewing the legality of Executive detention."[32] The fulcrum of the opinion, is a passage in which he points out that the writ of habeas corpus "does not act upon the prisoner who seeks relief, but upon the person who holds him in what is alleged to be unlawful custody."[33] In other words the question is not "Is Rasul within reach of the U.S. courts?" but "Is President Bush within reach of the United States courts?" The answer to that question is yes. Justice Stevens closes the opinion by again stating that the issue is not whether foreign nationals and the zone of Guantánamo stand within the penumbra of the law but whether President Bush does: "What is presently at stake is only whether the federal courts have jurisdiction to determine the legality of the Executive's potentially indefinite detention of individuals who claim to be wholly innocent of wrongdoing."[34] The answer, again: yes.

Two years later the Supreme Court examined the legitimacy of the military tribunals President Bush designed for Guantánamo, tribunals in which—as petitioner Salim Ahmed Hamdan complained—the accused is "excluded from his own trial."[35] The Court agreed: the tribunals violate what Justice Stevens, writing for the majority, identified as "the right to be present"—"one of the most fundamental protections."[36] A "glaring" feature of the tribunal design was its provision that the accused and his civilian counsel could be prohibited from hearing the evidence against him; a second feature was its inclusion of forms of evidence normally excluded—hearsay, information extracted by coercion, and testimony that was not sworn.[37]

The President's tribunals, the Court ruled, are illegal. Their design lacks any legislative authorization and violates both the Uniform Code of Military Justice and Common Article 3 of the Geneva Conventions. In the earlier case, *Rasul v. Bush*, the Geneva accords had been repeatedly mentioned in the oral arguments (and twice referred to as "the supreme law of the land") but had not been part of the decision itself.[38] Now in *Hamdan v. Rumsfeld* Common Article 3 provided the foundation for the Court's ruling. Among Common Article 3's provisions is the requirement that a defendant be tried "by a regularly constituted court affording all the judicial guarantees which are recognized as indispensable by civilized peoples." The requirement of a regularly constituted court is quoted eight times by Justice Stevens and thirteen times by Justice Kennedy in his concurring opinion.[39]

Responding to the President's long-standing complaint that Geneva rules are vague, Justice Stevens observed that in order to accommodate many different legal systems, the Geneva Conventions are broad and flexible in their requirements. "But *requirements* they are nonetheless."[40] Justice Kennedy similarly stressed the meaning of the word "requirement." When the United States ratified the Geneva Conventions, he noted, they became "binding law" in this country; moreover, he continued, as a result of Congress's 1996 War Crimes Act, a violation of Common Article 3 is "a war crime."[41]

In explaining what a "regularly constituted court" is, Justice Stevens and Justice Kennedy both invoked the definition given by the International Red Cross: a court "established and organized in accordance with the laws and procedures already in force in a country."[42] For detainees at Guantánamo, that would mean the court martial procedures established by the 1950 Uniform Code of Military Justice, or some other legislative base not yet provided by Congress.[43] The executive-branch contention that it would be "hamstrung" by the procedures of a military court martial is dismissed as insupportable by Justice Stevens, who repeatedly faults the government for its "wholesale jettisoning of procedural protections."[44] Hamdan may, as the government argues, be extremely dangerous, concludes Justice Stevens, "but in undertaking to try Hamdan . . . the Executive is bound to comply with the Rule of Law."[45]

Justice Kennedy comments on the odd necessity, apparently felt by Justice Stevens and him, to announce basic principles of international and national law (as though they were addressing a visitor from outer space), such as the fact just noted that following the rule of law is obligatory and that the legislative, executive, and judicial branches cannot act beyond the powers conferred on them by the Constitution.[46] But the main rebuke to the executive is the stark invocation of the Geneva rules and the reminder that their violation constitutes a "war crime." In January 2002 President Bush decided that Guantánamo detainees were not eligible for Geneva-rules protection; he later announced that he had the power to suspend them in Afghanistan but for the time being would not do so. In *Hamdan v. Rumsfeld*, the Court reminded the President and the American people that the Geneva rules had never ceased to be in effect, and that their violation is a war crime.

As the President's mock-judicial schemes have been addressed and corrected in *Rasul v. Bush* and *Hamdan v. Rumsfeld* (as well as in *Hamdi v. Rumsfeld* and *Boumediene v. Bush*), it is to be hoped that the U.S. courts will eventually try President Bush for direct acts of licensing torture. A remarkable step in this direction took place on August 14, 2008, when a federal appeals court in New York agreed *sua sponte* (on their own initiative, without a request from either party) to rehear the rendition and torture case *Arar v. Ashcroft*. The court, presided over by three of its twelve judges, had earlier dismissed the case on national security grounds. Maher Arar—a Canadian citizen arrested at JFK airport without charge, held in solitary confinement for two weeks, flown to Syria where he was tortured, and imprisoned in a three-foot by six-foot by seven-foot underground cell for a year—will have his case reheard by all twelve judges of the United States Court of Appeals for the Second Circuit on December 9, 2008.

Some of the evidence for other torture cases may well come from the executive branch itself. Beginning in spring 2002, FBI agents in Afghanistan, who witnessed the torture of Abu Zubayda by the military and the CIA, expressed alarm to their headquarters. By fall 2002 (a year before the worst abuses in Abu Ghraib, and a year and a half before those abuses were made public) FBI agents' continuing distress regarding military interrogation practices at Guantánamo had reached Attorney General Ashcroft and the Criminal Division of the Department of Justice.[47] The conflict between the FBI and the military became most intense over the interrogation of al-Qahtani and Mohamedou Ould Slahi.[48] In both cases, the aversive interrogation procedures were directly approved by Secretary of Defense Rumsfeld. The FBI and the Immigration and Naturalization Service, through fingerprints and timing, had discovered al-Qahtani's role in the events of 9/11, but at Guantánamo the military was subjecting al-Qahtani to forms of questioning that were not only prohibited by the FBI on moral and legal grounds (it allows only "rapport based" techniques), but would surely ruin any chance of getting actual information.[49]

Although a formal system of reporting within the FBI only began after the Abu Ghraib revelations, an elaborate survey of one thousand FBI agents carried out by the Office of the Inspector General at the Department of Justice in 2005 documented the agents' early and ongoing alarm, as well as their largely ineffective attempts to address it. The roughly 400-page *A Review of the FBI's Involvement in and Observations of Detainee Interrogations in Guantánamo Bay, Afghanistan, and Iraq* is important for its record of cruelties, both inside and outside the interrogation room.[50]

What the study chronicles, however, is not only cruelty but also a kind of cognitive anarchy across the three geographies of Guantánamo, Afghanistan, and Iraq. FBI agents were completely clear about what kinds of deeds had to be reported if carried out by an FBI agent: criminal acts, misconduct, or any act that might be perceived by someone else, and later reported, as misconduct. They also understood their "obligation to report" the actions of non-FBI government employees if the act was criminal (an obligation all government employees have under federal law).[51] Following the Abu Ghraib revelations, agents were instructed that if they saw a person exceeding not the FBI interrogation rules, as in the past, but the rules governing the body to which that person belonged—whether military or the CIA—they were obliged to report that as well.[52]

But what were the rules governing those other bodies? The FBI agents did not know, and constantly emailed headquarters to ask what constituted "abuse."[53] Perhaps because the secretary of defense had issued six different sets of rules, the soldiers posted at U.S. foreign detention centers also did not know, though they cheerfully thought they did and repeatedly assured FBI agents that the events underway were legal: an FBI agent walking through a corridor at Abu Ghraib and seeing men in cells wearing only underwear (a violation of Geneva rules) was assured by a sergeant escorting him that their nudity was authorized; 47 separate FBI agents either saw or were told about sleep deprivation yet were informed that this was standard, approved military procedure; FBI agents present at Abu Zubayda's initial CIA interrogations were told that the procedures being used had been approved "at the highest levels."[54]

The cognitive anarchy documented in the FBI *Review* again underscores the important phenomenon of transmissible authority. We saw earlier that a president's lying about another country is far more criminal in its consequence than the lying of an ordinary citizen because it is a lie that will be transmitted across millions of people and because it may authorize the widespread infliction of injury and death. So, too, the White House's decision to lift the prohibition on torture was transmitted to tens of thousands of soldiers who repeated false sentences about the suspendability of the Geneva Conventions and believed themselves authorized to practice once-forbidden acts. Even the thousand FBI agents who would in the past have had the means to stop torture, lost their bearings and did not know what to report.[55]

An Extra-legal Universe

President Bush's assault on the rule of law has thus been devastatingly effective. But it is challengeable, and those challenges may come from a range of Americans and domestic offices. It is also challengeable in international arenas. An array of international legal challenges have already been issued against members of the executive branch who carried out President Bush's program of "extraordinary rendition," a process in which individuals were seized and flown to countries (often those with a history of practicing torture) to be detained and interrogated. In January 2007 German prosecutors in Munich issued arrest warrants for thirteen CIA agents who allegedly participated in the kidnapping and imprisonment of German citizen Khaled al-Masri.[56] The following month, an Italian judge ordered the arrest and trial of 25 CIA agents who allegedly kidnapped Osama Mustafa Hassan Nasr on a Milan street and flew him to Egypt to be interrogated.[57] Studies carried out by the European Parliament—one completed in November 2006 and another in February 2007—have documented the 1,245 CIA flights that traveled through European airspace or made stopovers at European airports in the period between October 2001 and November 2006. In February 2007 the Parliament voted to condemn extraordinary rendition and urged the 27 member states of the European Union to continue their investigations and documentation of all flights.[58]

According to Sands, who has participated in international cases against government officials who torture, a case against President Bush or other members of his administration may be brought in an international forum. Citing Spain's demand that England extradite former Chilean leader Augusto Pinochet for crimes he had committed 22 years earlier, Sands suggests how probable such a scenario is if the United States itself fails to confront the grave crimes carried out by the administration and if Bush or Cheney travel to, or through, other countries in the near or even distant future.[59]

The Bush administration has dedicated itself to creating an alternative universe, an offshore world with no legal constraints on the American executive. Creating this universe has required fabricating stories and details, like the made-up account of nuclear weapons and the made-up account of Iraq's connection to al Qaeda, and the made-up sources and dossiers for this made-up information. Ever effective at generating false information, torture has also been used to produce these fictions. Sometimes the interrogators wore fake uniforms and flew a false national flag. The administration has also falsified body counts and accounts of injury and suppressed genuine accounts.[60] This fabricated universe also requires fabricating rules about habeas corpus in order to ensure that this made-up universe lies beyond the reach of real-world courts.

What has not been fabricated, however, are the injuries and deaths. *The New England Journal of Medicine* counts the number of dead Iraqi civilians at 151,000; in October 2006 the British medical journal *Lancet* placed the number at more than 650,000. The number, though uncertain, is real and large. The number of U.S. soldiers who have fallen as of August 18, 2008 is 4,145. The number of U.S. soldiers sent home with grave injuries is 13,453; another 17,056 less severely injured have remained on foreign soil.[61] The number of people tortured is not at present known, but, again, the number is real. It may seem surprising that a fabricated universe can bring about devastating injury, but, of course, it is exactly the purpose of the real world system of laws to prohibit such injuries, so it is not surprising that fabricated worlds lead to widespread bodily harm.

The avenues of address that have been outlined above may seem inadequate to the harm done. Will the Congressional articles of impeachment remain stuck in the Judiciary Committee? Will the Justice

Department appoint a special counsel to investigate the White House's authorization of torture? Will any state's attorney general answer Bugliosi's call to prosecute President Bush for the deaths of U.S. soldiers? Will other towns join Brattleboro and Marlboro by drafting and publishing their own indictments and arrest warrants, thus transforming the Brattleboro-Marlboro symbols into profound safeguards against future executive wrongdoing? Will the Second Circuit Court of Appeals hear *Arar v. Ashcroft* without this time allowing national security claims to silence the case? Will the United States extradite the thirteen who have been indicted in Germany for their part in the rendition of a German citizen? Will Belgium reinstate the "universal jurisdiction" statute it repealed when Rumsfeld threatened to have NATO headquarters moved because a Belgian court had agreed to hear a war crimes case brought by a group of injured and bereaved Iraqi civilians?

"How long won't you stand for injustice?" asks Bertolt Brecht's Mother Courage. If you're going to get tired after half an hour, she advises, or after a week, or after a month, you might as well leave right now. Mother Courage storms into a military headquarters to lodge a complaint, and, finding a young lieutenant there who is waiting to make his own complaint, she launches into her disquisition on the impossible fortitude and stamina required, and does this so effectively that she persuades herself. She promptly leaves without lodging any complaint. The event takes place shortly after the military execution, without trial, of her soldier-son.

Part of what makes the thought of prosecuting Bush so aversive is that it would be utterly exhausting. Bush has repeatedly short-circuited protest against one outrageous illegality by quickly carrying out a second, third, fourth, and fifth, so that the citizenry is kept in a permanent state of astonishment and cannot recover its ground long enough to do more than cry out. Now, at the end of his administration, the sheer number of accumulated wrongful acts disempowers the collective will to act, and tempts us to elect our way back into a legal order and simply close the door on the revolting spectacle of the last eight years.

But is closing the door actually an option? If the country is to renew its commitment to the rule of law, that outcome will require reeducating ourselves about what the law is. The law aspires to symmetry across cases. Among the more than two million Americans in prison and jail in 2006 was a young woman, Lynndie England, whose smiling face was photographed at Abu Ghraib as she held a dog leash attached to the neck of a naked prisoner. Yet no one is in prison for the crimes committed at Guantánamo, where direct White House agency has been elaborately documented, and where the long list of practices includes "tying a dog leash to detainee's chain, walking him around the room and leading him through a series of dog tricks."[62] How long won't you stand for injustice?

The legal memos to and from the White House have no power to alter the national and international rules against torture. Geneva rules state that they cannot be suspended in wartime, and a country can only withdraw from the accords in peacetime with a one year lead-time. Though the definition of torture in the Convention Against Torture is 118 words long, it has only "two key elements" that must be present: "that the act intentionally cause severe suffering and that it have official sanction."[63] The legal memos back and forth among the White House, the Secretary of Defense, and the Office of Legal Counsel, far from minimizing the crime of torture, fulfill its definitional requirements by verifying that it was done with "official sanction."

Finally—and for us, most important—the international rules against war crimes and torture do not allow prosecution to be thought of as discretionary; they do not allow an escape provision based on electoral euphoria or on one's doubts about one's own stamina in fighting injustice. Very distant from a mere disinclination to prosecute is a country's act of granting an amnesty. The international laws about some criminal acts do, in fact, allow for amnesty if required to establish peace. But torture is not one of those crimes. As Michael Scharf writes, the Commentary to the Geneva Conventions (the "official history" of their adoption) "confirms that the obligation to prosecute is 'absolute,' meaning . . . that states parties can under no circumstances grant perpetrators immunity or amnesty from prosecution for grave breaches."[64] So, too, the Convention against Torture requires that states "submit" cases to the "competent authorities for the purpose of prosecution."[65] This means, writes Scharf, that "where persons under color of law commit acts of torture in a country that is a party to the Torture Convention, the Convention requires Prosecution."[66]

The United States is a party to these agreements. The duty to prosecute means that the failure of a government to do so violates international law and that the country reneges on its treaty obligations.[67] It also increases the pressure of other countries to bring cases against Bush, Cheney, and Rumsfeld based on the principle of "universal jurisdiction" that permits all parties to a treaty to prosecute grave war crimes that originated in another country.

It is odd that the designers of the Brattleboro resolution used "universal jurisdiction" as one of its legal bases, since that doctrine exists to enable countries distinct from the wrongdoers' home ground to indict and arrest them. It is also odd that New York City's Center for Constitutional Rights, which in 2004 successfully argued for Guantánamo detainees to be heard in federal court, a year later chose to file a torture case by Iraqi prisoners against Rumsfeld in Germany rather than in the United States. The Center chose Germany because that country has an explicit statute permitting it to try war crimes carried out anywhere in the world if the home country neglects to do so. The logic both in Vermont and New York seems to be: if the doctrine of universal jurisdiction allows citizens of a different country to try a case, surely it authorizes citizens of the home country to do so.

Perhaps the valiant Brattleboro citizens and the stern fighters at the Center for Constitutional Rights doubt whether the ground they stand on is still in the United States. Can the ground be put back under their feet? How long?

Notes

Introduction

[1] United States Government Accountability Office Report to Congressional Requesters, *Homeland Defense: Actions Needed to Improve Management of Air Sovereignty Alert Operations to Protect U.S. Airspace*. Washington, D.C.: Government Publishing Office, January 2009. (Hereafter: *Actions Needed*.)

[2] On September 14, 2001, the Department of Defense introduced its new homeland air surveillance program, Operation NOBLE EAGLE. The Department's identification of the protection of the homeland as its primary goal also occurs in its 2005 *Strategy for Homeland Defense and Civil Support* and again in its 2008 *National Defense Strategy* (*Actions Needed*).

[3] When the GAO showed the Department of Defense a draft copy of its report, the Department at once concurred with the

central recommendation "to implement"—however belatedly—"[Air Sovereignty Alert] as a steady-state mission" (GAO, Actions Needed, p. 35). But it abstained from endorsing specific recommendations for bringing about that implementation and remained silent on the question of a timetable. The GAO report accordingly ends with an expression of dismay: "The Department of Defense's response further demonstrates the lack of consistency and clarity of concepts, definitions, and terms surrounding air sovereignty alert (ASA) we identified in our review" (Actions Needed).

4 In contrast to our unshielded soldiers, Dick Cheney each day traveled the residential streets of Washington, D.C. "chauffeured in an armored motorcade" (Mayer, J. 2008. *The Dark Side: The Inside Story of How The War on Terror Turned into a War on American Ideals*. New York: Doubleday).

5 Changes have been made in places where my editors found the phrasing particularly inelegant. My thanks to Simon Waxman and Deb Chasman.

6 George Bush began to use "offshore" geography even before 9/11. See David Barstow and Don Van Natta, Jr., "How Bush Took Florida: Mining the Overseas Absentee Vote," The New York Times, January 15, 2001. Barstow and Van Natta document the way ballots with late postmarks (or even no postmarks) from military ships and overseas bases were accepted if arriving late in Republican counties in Florida and rejected if arriving in Democratic counties. *The Times* devoted more than five full pages to the microscopic research that reviewed the postmarks on thousands of offshore ballots and built an elaborate database.

7 See Scahill, J. 2007. *Blackwater: the Rise of the World's Most*

Powerful Mercenary Army. New York: Nation Books. Scahill provides an account of the legal immunity of Blackwater forces in Iraq and other geographies, as well as their license to bypass all chains of military and civilian command; they reported directly to the White House.

[8] In the United States, prosecutors ordinarily *do* have great discretionary power over whether or not to prosecute a crime. Torture is an exception.

[9] For example, the November 2009 statement from the International Center for Transitional Justice.

Chapter 1

[1] R. Bhaskar, who urged me to read the Patriot Act soon after it was passed, made this observation about sufficiency.

[2] For a complete chronological list of the towns and states that have passed resolutions, as well as the text of each resolution, see the Web site of the Bill of Rights Defense Committee at www.bordc.org. Quoted passages from the resolutions throughout this essay are cited from this Web site.

[3] Bush, G. W. November 2001. "Presidential Military Order: Detention, Treatment, and Trial of Certain Non-Citizens in the War Against Terrorism," *Federal Register* 66 (222): 57,833–57,836. Department of Justice, Interim Rule. October 2001. "National Security; Prevention of Acts of Violence and Terrorism," *Federal Register* 66 (211): 55,062–55,066.

[4] For these reports, as well as denials by government officials, see Don Van Natta Jr., "Questioning Terror Suspects in a Dark and Surreal World," *The New York Times*, March 9, 2003 and Dana

Priest and Barton Gellman, "U.S. Decries Abuse but Defends Interrogations," *The Washington Post*, December 26, 2002. The information from Bagram and Diego Garcia includes reports that prisoners were forced to wear black hoods, subjected to extreme temperatures, forced into painful postures for many hours, kept naked, deprived of sleep, hung by their hands from the ceiling, withheld painkillers despite serious injuries such as a gunshot wound in the groin, and questioned in a building flying a false flag. Even in Guantánamo Bay, where interrogation procedures are believed to be less abusive, twenty have attempted suicide. Ten U.S. security officials were among those who gave such reports.

[5] For an analysis of the ways in which the Patriot Act revises earlier law, see the charts and fact sheets prepared by the American Civil Liberties Union at http://action.aclu.org/reformthepatriotact/.

[6] Controversial provisions of the Patriot Act are braided together with unobjectionable one, such as Title VI, which arranges for financial support for the families of public officers who were victims of terrorism.

[7] See Fried, C. 1968. "Privacy." *Yale Law Journal* 77: 475–482.

[8] Karst, K. L. "Right of Privacy." In Levy, L. W., Karst, K., and Mahoney, D. (Eds.). 1990. *Encyclopedia of the American Constitution*. New York: Macmillan. Karst, K. L. 1980. "The Freedom of Intimate Association." *Yale Law Journal* 89 (624).

[9] As the local resolution of Evanston, Illinois, summarizes it, "Privacy is essential to the exercise of free speech, free thought and free association."

[10] The Constitution includes a secrecy provision for Congres-

sional proceedings (it has no similar provision for the executive or judicial branches).

[11] The Constitution envisions the president executing (rather than making or issuing) laws and therefore does not require the president to record the deliberations that led to his making or issuing a law. When the president sees the need for new legislation, he will (according to I, 3) report that need to Congress, which will then go on to consider the creation of that legislation and record the proceedings in their journal.

[12] Sunstein, C. 1986. "New Perspectives in the Law of Defamation." *California Law Review* 74: 889–897. See also Meiklejohn, A. 1948. *Free Speech and Its Relation to Self-Government.* New York: Harper & Row.

[13] The section pertaining to the monitoring of private records that is most frequently cited in local resolutions is section 215—often the only section explicitly mentioned by number. At the other extreme are cities such as Ashland, Oregon, which lists all of the sections enumerated here except for section 203 (which is included in Ann Arbor's July 2003 postscript to its original resolution). In the period between the passage of the first resolution—Ann Arbor's, on January 7, 2002—and Septmber 2004 (when this article was originally published), the resolutions tended to provide an increasingly complete analysis, acting as readers' guides to the Patriot Act. See also, for example, the lucid examination by Brookline, Massachusetts. In their thoughtfulness and passion, the local resolutions collectively recall the pamphlet wars in the time of the Constitution.

[14] Michael T. McCarthy reminds us that at the time the Patriot Act was going through Congress, the Senate was partially closed

down due to the anthrax scare: McCarthy, M. 2002. "Recent Development: U.S.A. Patriot Act." *Harvard Journal on Legislation* 39(2).

[15] The impassioned Oroville, Washington, resolution uses similar phrasing, though it does not speak of martial law.

[16] Closely related is the 1976 case *Mathews v. Diaz*, which upheld the extension of the Bill of Rights to illegal aliens.

[17] *Securities Industry News*, May 27, 2002.

[18] "New Anti-Money Laundering Programs." 2002. *The Review of Securities & Commodities Regulation.* Geoffrey Connor observes that a rule of thumb emerges: "When in doubt, file a suspicious activity report," (Connor, G. 2002. *New Jersey Law Journal* 29). The Patriot Act grants safe harbor to other citizens who are asked to turn over records. For example, section 507, in a subsection on "Disclosure of Education Records," states, "An educational agency or institution that, in good faith, produces education records in accordance with an order issued under this subsection shall not be liable to any person for that production." Sections 215 and 508 similarly provide "safe harbor" to citizens who assist the executive branch in intelligence gathering.

[19] A lengthened list was issued on December 17, 2002.

[20] Massachusetts Institute of Technology. June 2002. "In the Public Interest: Report of the Ad Hoc Faculty Committee on Access to and Disclosure of Scientific Information." As the report notes, the Patriot Act imposes criminal penalties only on individual violators of its rule, but pending legislation extends the criminal penalties to institutions.

[21] MIT. "In the Public Interest." MIT does permit classified re-

search in off-campus sites such as Draper Laboratory and Lincoln Laboratory.

[22] MIT. "In the Public Interest." Like the local resolutions, the MIT report not only defends but celebrates the presence of foreign nationals within the university walls: "Openness enables MIT to attract, educate, and benefit from the best students, faculty and staff from around the world. . . . access to research and knowledge outside the United States is critical to our own progress. Over the course of many years, immigrant scientists as well as foreign visitors and students have contributed enormously to the American educational and scientific enterprises. . . . No foreign national granted a visa by the United States government should be denied access to courses, research or publications generally available on campus."

[23] They worked through Wisconsin Democratic Senator Russell Feingold, the only senator who voted against the Patriot Act.

[24] See the American Library Association's richly informative Web site: http://www.ala.org/ala/issuesadvocacy/advocacy/federallegislation/theusapatriotact/index.cfm.

[25] Starting in November 2001 (less than a month after the bill's passage), notice appeared in the *Portland [Maine] Press Herald, El Paso Times, The Hartford Courant, San Jose Mercury News, [Arlington Heights, Illinois] Daily Herald, St. Louis Post-Dispatch, Daily Oklahoman, [Dubuque, Iowa] Telegraph Herald,* and scores of others.

[26] Dan Eggen, "Ashcroft Derides Patriot Act Critics," *The Washington Post,* September 19, 2003 and Eric Lichtblau, "Ashcroft Mocks Librarians and Others Who Oppose Parts of Counterterrorism Law," *The New York Times,* September 16, 2003.

ELAINE SCARRY   167

[27] Mao Tse-Tung, for example, was a librarian in 1918 when he worked under "the chief librarian of Peking University, who was one of the pioneer Marxists of China" (*Encyclopedia of World Biography*. Edition 2, Volume 18. Detroit: Gale Research, 1998).

[28] Adam Clymer, "THREATS AND RESPONSES: PRIVACY; Librarians Get Advice on Handling Government Requests for Information on Readers," *The New York Times*, December 12, 2002. A follow-up study of Illinois libraries alone found no libraries contacted, but the national figures of 4 percent and 11 percent still stand. (Interview with University of Illinois Professor and Dean of Library and Information Science Leigh S. Estabrook. November 2, 2003.) The follow-up study also found that 29 percent of public libraries and 16 percent of academic libraries now have written procedures in place to guide librarians who are presented with a search warrant or a subpoena (Amanda Vogt, *Chicago Tribune*, December 18, 2003). On the history of FBI inquiries into library records before 9/11, see the detailed account of Herbert N. Foerstel, a retired University of Maryland librarian (Foerstel, H. N. 1991. *Surveillance in the Stacks*, Westport, CT: Greenwood Press). Foerstel traces the FBI's many self-righteous denials of library surveillance, the librarians' own record of FBI visits, and the 3,000 pages of FBI documents that eventually surfaced with the help of the Freedom of Information Act.

[29] In October 2001 Attorney General Ashcroft sent a memo to many government departments telling them that if they declined to answer Freedom of Information Act requests, the Justice Department would support them. The draft of Patriot Act II ("Domestic Security Enhancement Act of 2003") seeks to increase the Department of Justice's own exemption from Freedom of Information Act rules. Section 201 complains of having to go

through time-consuming court procedures to defend the Act's withholding of information about detainees, time better spent tracking down terrorists. It asks for explicit authority to regularly withhold information about detainees until after criminal charges are pressed.

[30] To the five steps outlined above, Attorney General Ashcroft added a sixth on his sixteen-day tour: claim that you're not actually using the legislation (as in the case of section 215) while simultaneously claiming that it is only because you have been using this excellent tool extensively that the country has not had more terrorist attacks since 9/11.

[31] Many sections of the Patriot Act conflate crime and terrorism (for example, sections 203, 403, 405, 413, 813), allowing the Department of Justice to use all the tools against each in its pursuit of the other, while also—as in the case of Bill Olds—playing a shell game with the public to hide its own actions and prohibit any protest.

[32] Bill Olds, "The FBI Has Bugged Our Private Libraries," *The Hartford Courant*, November 3, 2002; "FBI Searched Library Computer, Didn't Install Monitoring Program; Claim Made in Sunday Courant Was Wrong, Columnist Says," *The Hartford Courant*, November 7, 2002; "Letters to the Editor," *The Hartford Courant*, November 8, 2002; Karen Hunter, "Anonymous Sources, Bad Information," *The Hartford Courant*, November 10, 2002; "Damaged Credibility," *The Hartford Courant*, November 12, 2002; See also *The Hartford Courant*, November 17, 2002; "Did FBI Bug Hartford Library? Nope," *Library Journal*, November 11, 2002; "Late Bulletins," *Library Journal*, December 15, 2002; Interview with Bill Olds. December 18, 2002 and January 4, 2003; Interview with Karen Hunter, December 19, 2002.

[33] Sometimes, as in the case of Seattle, the resolution will arrange for the public posting of the Bill of Rights.

[34] Alternatively, the local resolution may, as in Woodstock, New York, advise librarians and local businesspeople to "refrain . . . from keeping records which identify the purchaser or borrower"; or, as in San Mateo, California, may support House Resolution 1157, the "Freedom to Read Protection Act of 2003," to exempt libraries and bookstores from inclusion in the Patriot Act.

[35] When the locality itself possesses the information, it is directed to make that information available: the resolutions of Oxford, Ohio, and Rio Arriba, New Mexico, for example, direct universities and secondary schools to inform any student whose record has been seized by the federal government.

[36] Intelligence-gathering is acceptable, observes Denver, only if it is "regularly and rigorously examined for compliance" with the Constitution.

[37] Some localities, such as Madison, Wisconsin, urge that the entire Act be repealed.

[38] The "police" are almost always explicitly named. Other professions are sometimes named—as in Provincetown, Massachusetts's explicit instruction to librarians—but are more often covered by the general rubric "town employees."

[39] David Cole, "Enemy Aliens and American Freedoms: Why Sacrificing Immigrants' Rights in the War on Terrorism Undermines Our Security and Our Liberty." Lecture delivered at Harvard Law School, September 24, 2003. Two of the four were acquitted. Of the two to whom charges stuck, one was found guilty of trying to dismantle the Brooklyn Bridge with an acetylene torch.

[40] "Self-interest," though certainly threatened by the Patriot Act, does not appear to distinguish the Patriot Act from other forms of executive action. As the worldwide loss of affection for the American people attests, it is against the population's self-interest for their country to carry out executive-driven wars based on false information, detain 5,000 immigrants and foreign visitors without charges, and torture prisoners.

[41] Nat Hentoff, a tireless critic of the Patriot Act and other post-9/11 abridgments of rights, also points out the resemblance between the Patriot Act search powers and the Writs of Assistance on the basis of "generality" (Nat Hentoff, "'Sneak and peek': The House rejects funds for Patriot provision," *The Washington Times*, August 4, 2003). See also: Hentoff, N. 2003. *The War on the Bill of Rights and the Gathering Resistance*. San Francisco: Seven Stories Press.

[42] Adams, J. "Letter to William Tudor. March 29, 1817." In Adams, C. F. (Ed.). 1856. *The Life and Works of John Adams, Vol. 10*. Boston: Little, Brown, and Co.

[43] Blue, J. C. 1992. "*High Noon* Revisited: Commands of Assistance by Peace Officers in the Age of the Fourth Amendment." *The Yale Law Journal* 101(7): 1475–1490. My thanks to Akhil Amar for directing my attention to Judge Blue's ruling.

[44] Warren, M. O. 1988. *History of the Rise, Progress, and Termination of the American Revolution, Volume 1*. Indianapolis: Liberty Classics. See also: Adams, J. In Adams, C. F. (Ed.). *The Life and Works of John Adams, Volume 10*.

[45] Penalties may fall on individuals, towns, or states. U.S. Representative Tom Tancredo proposed an amendment to the 2004 Appropriations Act (H.R. 2555, 108th Congress) that would with-

hold federal funding from any town or state that refuses to provide federal officers information about an individual's citizenship or immigration status. The amendment was defeated, 322 to 102.

46 On the floor of the Senate, Senator Feingold gave just this interpretation of the Justice Department's sudden defensiveness. *Reasonable Notice and Search Act*, S 1701, 108th Cong., 1st sess., *Congressional Record* 149 (October 2, 2003): S 12377.

47 The Bush Administration has tended to proceed on the basis that no explanations are needed. Indeed, President Bush stated to Bob Woodward in an interview, "I'm the commander—see, I don't need to explain—I do not need to explain why I say things. That's the interesting thing about being the president" (Woodward, B. 2003. *Bush at War*. New York: Simon and Schuster). Attorney General Ashcroft's sixteen-city tour to address local police and prosecutors reminds us that local law enforcers do not simply follow orders but must be individually convinced of the justness of the law they are being asked to uphold, especially if it appears to violate Constitutional law.

48 This summary of the vote was made by Representative Bernie Sanders (I-VT), a fierce opponent of the Patriot Act, especially section 215.

49 S 1552, 108th Congress, sponsored by Senator Lisa Murkowski (R-AK) and co-sponsored by Senator Ron Wyden (D-OR).

50 *Security and Freedom Ensured Act of 2003 (SAFE Act)*, S 1709, 108th Congress, sponsored by Senator Larry Craig (R-ID).

51 S 1695, 108th Congress, sponsored by Senator Patrick Leahy (D-VT).

52 S 436, 108th Congress, sponsored by Senator Patrick Leahy.

[53] S 1507, 108th Congress, sponsored by Senator Russell Feingold (D-WI).

[54] S 609, 108th Congress, sponsored by Senator Patrick Leahy.

[55] "Hearing of the Senate Committee on the Judiciary on Criminal Terrorism Investigations and Prosecutions," October 21, 2003, chaired by Senator Orrin Hatch (R-UT). The November installment of the hearings was on "Post–September 11th Civil Rights Issues."

[56] December 8, 2003, "Conference Report on H.R. 2673, Consolidated Appropriations Act, 2004," 149 Congressional Record House 12766 (vol.149, no. 175). Kucinich was a co-sponsor of the amendment.

[57] During the October 21, 2003 Congressional hearings on the Patriot Act, Senator Diane Feinstein reported that her mail on the Patriot Act was 21,434 letters against and six letters in favor. According to Feinstein, many of the negative letters, though ostensibly addressed to the content of the first Patriot Act, more accurately describe the extreme provisions arranged for in Patriot Act II. While Patriot Act II has never been brought before Congress, the Bush administration has tried to embed various clauses inside other bills, such as a clause allowing the FBI (without court approval) to require records from more businesses than had been included in the original Patriot Act. This provision was folded into the 2004 Intelligence Authorization Act, approved by Congress in November 2003. While the bill did pass, the vote was much more split (263 to 163) than would have occurred without the provision, as an ACLU legislative counsel explains: "It prompted more than a third of the House, including 15 conservative Republicans, to change what is normally a cakewalk vote into something

truly contested" (Timothy Edgar, quoted by Jim Lobe in "Going Backwards: Patriot Act Expansion Moves Through Congress," *Inter Press Service*, November 21, 2003).

[58] Siobhan Roth, writing in *New Jersey Law Journal* (December 29, 2003), gives examples: "the Second Circuit decided Nov. 7 that the government may hold material witnesses indefinitely and without charges for grand jury investigations"; "the D.C. Circuit ruled on June 17 that the Justice Department does not have to release the names of anyone detained in the post–Sept. 11 dragnet because of national security concerns"; "the Third and Sixth Circuits are split on whether immigration hearings must be open to the public, [and the] Supreme Court has declined to consider the issue."

[59] *The Wall Street Journal* announced that Bush "was dealt a setback"; *The New York Times* called them "twin blows" (Neil A. Lewis and William Glaberson, "U.S. Courts Reject Detention Policy in 2 Terror Cases," *The New York Times*, December 19, 2003.); *New York Law Journal* called them "stinging rebukes" (Mark Hamblett, "Panels See Limits in Bush's Antiterror Authority," *New York Law Journal*, December 19, 2003); *The Bergen Record* called them "direct" and "sweeping" rebukes.

[60] The Justice Department has justified holding the U.S. citizen José Padilla in a Navy prison without charge and without access to a lawyer by saying that President Bush, as commander in chief, had declared him "an enemy combatant"; the Second Circuit ruled that no citizen can be detained without due process unless explicitly authorized by Congress. The court concluded that Padilla was not, as asserted by the Bush administration, "captured" in a combat zone but was peaceably arrested on U.S. soil and must therefore be treated under rules written to address crime, not rules written for war.

[61] Padilla, in the Second Circuit ruling, and the foreign citizen Salim Gherebi (and by extension, all 660 detainees in Guantánamo Bay) in the Ninth Circuit ruling.

[62] The Second Circuit argued, "This case involves not whether [the responsibilities the president and law-enforcement officials bear for protecting the nation] should be aggressively pursued, but whether the president is obligated, in the circumstances presented here, to share them with Congress." The Ninth Circuit judges observed, "We share the desire of all Americans to ensure that the executive enjoys the necessary power and flexibility to prevent future terrorist attacks. However, even in times of emergency—indeed, particularly in such times—it is the obligation of the judicial branch to ensure the preservation of our Constitutional values and to prevent the executive branch from running roughshod over the rights of citizens and aliens alike" (David Stout, "Courts Deal Blow to Bush on Treatment of Terror Suspects," *The New York Times*, December 18, 2003).

Chapter 2

[1] Though there was a strong reaction to the initial reports of this incident, eventually it became clear that the suicide-bomber taxi driver had not in fact used a white flag.

[2] Rendition, like torture, is prohibited by the Geneva Conventions. Article 12 states that a signatory country can send prisoners only to other signatory countries; in transferring a prisoner, the first country has not transferred all responsibility.

[3] For example, in his January 19, 2002, memorandum to the chairman of the Joint Chiefs of Staff, Rumsfeld states that detainees are "not entitled to prisoner of war status for the purposes of the Geneva Conventions." Later, in his April 16, 2003,

memorandum to the commander of the U.S. Southern Command, he reiterates, "the provisions of Geneva are not applicable to unlawful combatants."

[4] This memorandum and many others are reproduced in two books of documents: Danner, M. 2004. *Torture and Truth: America, Abu Ghraib, and the War on Terror*. New York: New York Review Books and Greenberg, K. J. and Dratel, J. L. 2005. *The Torture Papers: The Road to Abu Ghraib*. New York: Cambridge University Press.

[5] This rule applies to nations with formal militaries and includes complicated exceptions for popular uprisings, resistance fighters, and guerilla fighters. During its consideration of "rules applicable in guerilla warfare" in a 1971 conference on international humanitarian law in armed conflict, members of the International Committee of the Red Cross worried about the way the absence of uniforms among these groups may, if fighters are taken prisoner, unfairly deprive them of prisoner-of-war status. The Red Cross notes that these groups are still required to "conduct their operations in accordance with laws and customs of war."

[6] It is reasonable to suppose that members of the military may have seen and voiced aloud their concerns about the trespass of rules. Often the civilian world learns belatedly, or not at all, of military objections to a country's undertakings: only in early March 2004, for example, did the public learn that British military leaders had, a year earlier, objected to invading Iraq without a second UN resolution for fear that they would be later convicted of war crimes. It is also crucial to remember that we would still know nothing of torture at Abu Ghraib were it not for one soldier—Specialist Joseph Darby—who understood (and stood by) the rules.

⁷ During the weeks immediately following the event, the hospital was referred to, inaccurately, as "Saddam Hussein Hospital."

⁸ So strong is this non-discrimination rule in the care of the sick that the Red Cross, which at one point had suggested that nurses in Red Cross hospitals be paired by nationality with patients when possible, later rescinded the recommendation.

⁹ The public record for this time does include a widely reported Iraqi misuse of a white flag. According to reports, on March 23, 2003, an Iraqi artillery unit near Nasiriyah displayed a white flag and then fired on and killed nine U.S. Marines. But by the end of the spring, the U.S. military acknowledged that these deaths were instead the result of American fratricide: an A-10 flying over the area misidentified, fired on, and killed the soldiers.

¹⁰ For more about these and other examples, see McDougal, M. S. and Feliciano, F. P. 1961. *Law and Minimum World Public Order: The Legal Regulation of International Coercion.* New Haven. CT: Yale University Press and Tucker, R. W. 1955. *The Law of War and Neutrality at Sea.* Washington, D.C.: United States Government Printing Office.

¹¹ Because torture so often produces false information, U.S. officials could not act on the information Zubayda gave them about the Saudi officials without validating it independently; their attempts to validate it failed, and Zubayda's information therefore proved useless.

¹² Though the prohibition against using the enemy's flag or uniform is today widely recognized in the United States as applying only to battle, there is at least one post–World War II regulation that asserts a blanket prohibition: Article 39 (2) of the 1977 Geneva Protocol. This blanket prohibition has been rejected by

the United States (see Matheson, M. 1987. "The United States Position on the Relation of Customary International Laws to the 1977 Protocols Additional to the 1949 Geneva Conventions." *American University Journal of International Law and Policy* 2(2): 419–431).

Some of the pre–World War II arguments on behalf of the blanket prohibition continue to have considerable force: one scholar of international law, for example, points out the oddity of limiting the prohibition against using deceptive identifying marks to the very moment when one's actions make one's allegiance entirely evident—when one is firing on the enemy.

Of course, the display of national affiliation during battle not only announces one's intention to do harm, but also acknowledges responsibility for the injuries that follow. How important this act of acknowledgment is has in recent years become increasingly clear with the appearance of weapons that are decoupled from any human agent (unmanned planes) or that carry no national signature (electromagnetic transmissions that affect equipment and people without leaving any trace of where the assault originated).

[13] In the immediate aftermath of 9/11, this approach was urged by international law experts such as Richard Faulk.

[14] Major Tyler J. Harder argues that Executive Order 12,333 should be eliminated because it is redundant given Hague 23(b) prohibitions, but he simultaneously argues that it should be eliminated to give the U.S. executive and military more flexibility, thus providing that on some level Executive Order 12,333 is an effective, and needed, second brake on assassination, even if it does repeat international protocols. (Maj. Harder, T. J. June 2002. "Time to Repeal the Assassination Ban of Executive Order

12,333: A Small Step in Clarifying Current Law." *Military Law Review* 172: 1–39.)

[15] A parallel instance of folksy Western phrasing appeared in President Bush's 2003 State of the Union address. After alluding to the arrest of 3,000 suspected al Qaeda terrorists, President Bush said, "And many others have met a different fate. Let's put it this way: they are no longer a problem to the United States and our friends and allies." Hendrik Hertzberg wrote, "You could almost see the president blowing across the upturned barrel of his Colt .45." (Hendrik Hertzberg, "Blixkrieg," *The New Yorker*. February 10, 2003.) Hertzberg complains that the sentences are "tasteless," but a problem more grave than taste appears to be involved.

[16] Threats against U.S. leaders are treated aggressively no matter how implausible or non-literal. In October 2006, a fourteen-year-old girl who had temporarily posted on MySpace the words "Kill Bush" and a picture of a knife pointing toward the president's outstretched hand was visited by two Secret Service men who came first to her home, then to her school. They removed her from her eighth-grade biology class and questioned her harshly, telling her that she could be sent to juvenile hall. (Associated Press, "Secret Service questions teen over Web threats," October 14, 2006.)

[17] Criminal law allows the posting of rewards and wanted signs, but not "wanted, dead or alive" announcements, since the alleged criminal must undergo a trial.

[18] For an account of the January 13, 2006 "attempt to assassinate al Qaeda second-in-command Ayman Zawahiri in Pakistan," using a top-secret program of unmanned Predator drones, see

Jane Meyer, "CIA Expands Uses of Drones in Terror War," *Los Angeles Times,* January 29, 2006. The attempt missed Zawahiri but killed eighteen civilians. Among those targeted and killed by predator drones were (according to the *Times*), the military commander Mohammed Atef in Afghanistan, Qaed Harithi in Yemen, Haitham Yemeni and Abu Hamza Rabia in Pakistan, and "a tall man in flowing robes" on the Pakistan-Afghanistan border who was wrongly thought to be Osama bin Laden. The Rabia killing included his seventeen-year-old son and the eight-year-old nephew of his landlord. The number of civilian deaths in the other targeted killings is not known.

[19] Parks, W. H. December 1989. "Memorandum of Law: Executive Order 12333 and-Assassination." *The Army Lawyer* (Department of the Army Pamphlet 27-50-204): 4–9; Schmitt, M. N. 1992. "State Sponsored Assassination in International and Domestic Law." *Yale Journal of International Law* 17: 609–685; and Maj. Harder, T. J. 2002. "Time to Repeal the Assassination Ban of Executive Order 12,333: A Small Step in Clarifying Current Law."

[20] Here Harder appears to have conflated the listing of assassination, rewards, and wanted announcements with the display of the red cross or white flag: it is indeed true to say that in war it is legal to shoot a gun at one's opponent but is treacherous to hold a white flag and shoot a gun at an opponent. But Harder concludes, using the foregoing as a template, that it must be legal to assassinate but treacherous to assassinate while holding a white flag (or otherwise enlisting the enemy's confidence). Were this an appropriate template, there would not be a need even to introduce the category of assassination, since the prohibition on assassinating while holding a white flag is already covered by the prohibition on the misuse of the white flag.

[21] Though I have suggested two grounds that show the incoherence of requiring a violation of confidence to make assassination illegal, this idea has some plausible precedents that Schmitt offers in his richly detailed historical overview.

[22] As Schmitt notes, a 1975 congressional investigation of attempted assassinations by the CIA records numerous attempts that certainly involved betrayal of confidence. For example, the Air Force Pamphlet (section 6.6d) says that one cannot injure enemy soldiers (or, needless to say, civilians) using objects enlisting confidence. The Air force's example is putting an explosive in a fountain pen. The CIA attempted to kill Fidel Castro in the early 1960s by placing a lethal toxin in a cigar, placing an explosive device in a rare seashell deep under water (Castro was known to be an expert diver and lover of beautiful shells), and arming a fountain pen with a hypodermic needed so fine that he would not notice the injection.

[23] The defense expert William Arkin, interviewed for a Discovery Channel documentary on Osama bin Laden, said that rewards offers are addressed to "close friends and associates."

[24] Though interrogators are permitted to wear false military uniforms, they are explicitly prohibited from wearing false Red Cross uniforms: the two forms of false signs that were coupled together in Article 23(f) of the Hague Conventions and the perfidy and treachery sections of the Air Force, Army, and Navy handbooks have therefore, in this new field manual, been decoupled from one another.

[25] Section 6.5 of the Air Force pamphlet continues with a set of cautionary sentences: "The weapons have been the subject of intense international political interest and international regula-

tion because of their potential for mass destruction, the historical fact of their recent development by only a very few powers with the ability to control their development and deployment, and international concern about possible proliferation." The section then lists the international treaties the United States has signed that may bear on the question of their use.

Chapter 3

[1] The town resolutions against the Patriot Act can be read on the Web site of the Bill of Rights Defense Committee: http://www.bordc.org.

[2] The town resolutions urging impeachment can be read at http://www.afterdowningstreet.org.

[3] Bugliosi, V. 2008. *The Prosecution of George W. Bush for Murder.* New York: Vanguard Press. Bugliosi is not unmindful of the horror of the Iraqi dead; the U.S. laws under which the case he outlines would be tried do not, however, accommodate foreign soldiers and civilians.

[4] A state-by-state list of the dead can be found on *The Washington Post* Web site: http://projects.washingtonpost.com/fallen.

[5] U.S. Senate. *Report on Whether Public Statements Regarding Iraq by U.S. Government Officials Were Substantiated by Intelligence Information.* 110th Congress. 2nd Session. Washington, D.C.: Government Publishing Office, June 2008. (Hereafter: *Senate Report.*)

[6] Ibid.

[7] Ibid.

[8] Ibid.

⁹ Mayer, J. 2008. *The Dark Side: The Inside Story of How The War on Terror Turned into a War on American Ideals.*

¹⁰ *Senate Report.*

¹¹ Ibid. Emphasis added.

¹² Dick Cheney. Speech delivered in Casper, Wyoming. September 20, 2002. Distributed by Associated Press, September 20, 2002; *Meet the Press*, March 16, 2003. Emphasis added. In an interview with Tim Russert, Cheney retracted his statement that Saddam Hussein "has, in fact, reconstituted nuclear weapons," but many more people saw Cheney's original speech than saw the interview (Interview with Dick Cheney. *Meet the Press.* September 14, 2003).

¹³ *Senate Report.*

¹⁴ Ibid.

¹⁵ In general, Colin Powell is much more careful to cite ambiguities and equivocations than are George Bush, Dick Cheney, or Condoleezza Rice. However, Powell will sometimes build from that position of acknowledged uncertainty to a climactic certainty that (precisely because of his willingness to be detailed and nuanced) ends up being dangerously compelling. In his UN speech in February 2003, he alludes to the uncertainty surrounding the aluminum tubes and then goes on to make their use in nuclear weapons sound certain. Again, with regard to the five-to-seven year window: in his September 26, 2002 testimony before the Senate he acknowledges the possibility that the completion of a weapon of mass destruction may be seven years away, but he also includes what is nowhere present in the intelligence, that it may be one day away: "They have not lost the intent to develop these weapons

of mass destruction, whether they are one day, five days, one year or seven years away from any particular weapon" (*Senate Report*).

[16] *Senate Report.*

[17] Ibid.

[18] *Report on Minority Views of Vice Chairman Bond and Senators Chambliss, Hatch, and Burr, attached to Senate Report.*

[19] This is not to say that the speakers repeating the president's words—a list that includes former presidential candidates Hillary Clinton, John Edwards, and John Kerry as well as John Rockefeller, the chair of the committee authoring the *Senate Report*—are wholly without fault. Some senators, hundreds of thousands of citizens, and many citizens of many other countries went on record saying no evidence warranting invasion had yet been given.

[20] Thus Bugliosi reminds us that in September 2001 a national poll showed that only 3 percent of the population mentioned Iraq as a possible participant in the events of 9/11; by August 2002, 70 percent of the population attributed responsibility to Iraq. So often was the lie repeated by the White House that even after President Bush eventually acknowledged that there was no evidence linking Iraq to 9/11, 43 percent of the population continued to believe Iraq was responsible; among troops in Iraq, the figure is 90 percent (Bugliosi, V. 2008. *The Prosecution of George W. Bush for Murder*).

[21] For example, a February 2007report issued by the Inspector General at the Department of Defense states that the Pentagon "inappropriately disseminated" an analysis linking Iraq to the al Qaeda 9/11 terrorists. Available intelligence had been "unable to substantiate" the link. The 2004 *Senate Report* examining the

accuracy of the pre-war intelligence noted, "the DoD policy office attempted to shape the CIA's terrorism analysis in late 2002 and, when it failed, prepared an alternative intelligence analysis denigrating the CIA for not embracing a link between Iraq and the 9/11 terrorist attacks." As later sections of this essay will indicate, the pressure to produce information about an al Qaeda–Iraq partnership appears to have involved the White House licensing of torture. This possibility is not included in the Senate Report, except in its account of al-Libi as described above.

[22] *Prewar Iraq Intelligence*, S 5135, 110th Cong., 2nd sess., *Congressional Record* (June 5, 2008).

[23] Bugliosi pursues both these matters in *The Prosecution of George W. Bush for Murder*.

[24] Waldron, J. 2005. "Torture and Positive Law: Jurisprudence for the White House." *Columbia Law Review* 105 (6).

[25] Sands, P. 2008. *Torture Team: Rumsfeld's Memo and the Betrayal of American Values*. New York: Palgrave Macmillan.

[26] "Final Report of the Independent Panel to Review DoD Detention Operations." In Danner, M. 2004. *Torture and Truth: America, Abu Ghraib, and the War on Terror*. New York Review Books: New York. In her interview with Major General Taguba, Karpinski cited the repeated visits of Deputy Secretary of Defense Paul Wolfowitz to Abu Ghraib, without indicating whether he was the official who conveyed the White House's keen interest in the interrogation results ("The Taguba Report: Article 15-6 Investigation of the 800th Military Police Brigade." In Greenberg, K. J. and Dratel, J. L. (Eds.). 2005. *The Torture Papers: the Road to Abu Ghraib*. Cambridge, U.K.: Cambridge University Press).

[27] Paust, J. J. 2007. "Above the Law: Unlawful, Executive Authorizations Regarding Detainee Treatment, Secret Renditions, Domestic Spying, and Claims to Unchecked Executive Power," *Utah Law Review* (2007): 345–419.

[28] Mark Mazzetti, "Ex-Pentagon Lawyers Face Inquiry on Interrogation Role," *The New York Times*, June 17, 2008.

[29] Joby Warrick, "Justice Dept. Urged to Examine Authorization of Harsh Interrogation Tactics," *The Washington Post*, June 7, 2008.

[30] Scott Shane, "Elusive Starting Point on Harsh Interrogations," *The New York Times*, June 11, 2008.

[31] Taguba, A. Preface to "Broken Laws, Broken Lives: Medical Evidence of Torture by US Personnel and Its Impact." 2008. Cambridge, Mass.; Washington, DC: Physicians for Human Rights.

[32] Justice John Paul Stevens, quoting the decision in *INS v. St. Cyr.*, 533 U.S. 289, 301 (2001) in *Shafiq Rasul, et al., Petitioners v. George W. Bush, President of the United States et al.*, (2004).

[33] Justice Stevens, quoting the decision in *Braden v. 30th Judicial Circuit Court of Ky.*, 421 U.S. 484, 495 (1973) in *Rasul v. Bush.*

[34] Justice Stevens, *Rasul v. Bush.*

[35] Justice Stevens, *Salim Ahmed Hamdan, Petitioner v. Donald H. Rumsfeld, Secretary of Defense, et al.*, (2006).

[36] Ibid.

[37] Ibid.

[38] Oral Arguments, *Rasul v. Bush*.

[39] Justice Stevens, *Hamdan v. Rumsfeld*.

[40] Ibid.

[41] Justice Anthony Kennedy, *Hamdan v. Rumsfeld*.

[42] Justice Stevens, *Hamdan v. Rumsfeld*; Justice Kennedy, *Hamdan v. Rumsfeld*.

[43] One might argue that all three legal grounds—the Geneva Conventions, the Uniform Code of Military Justice, and the absent Congressional legislation—provide equal foundations for *Hamdan v. Rumsfeld*. But as Justice Kennedy notes in his concurring opinion, the requirement to follow the court martial procedures of the UCMJ or to have Congress provide a legislative base are both themselves derived from the Geneva requirement for a "regularly constituted court" (Justice Kennedy, *Hamdan v. Rumsfeld*).

[44] Justice Stevens, *Hamdan v. Rumsfeld*. Stevens draws on Winthrop, W. 1920. *Military Law and Precedents,* 2nd ed.

[45] Justice Stevens, *Hamdan v. Rumsfeld*; Justice Kennedy, *Hamdan v. Rumsfeld*.

[46] Justice Kennedy, *Hamdan v. Rumsfeld*; Justice Stevens, *Hamdan v. Rumsfeld*.

[47] Office of the Inspector General, Oversight and Review Division, U.S. Department of Justice. 2008. *A Review of the FBI's Involvement in and Observations of Detainee Interrogations in Guantánamo Bay, Afghanistan, and Iraq.* (Hereafter: *Review of the FBI's Involvement.*)

[48] Ibid.

[49] Ibid. From 2002 onward an important voice in maintaining the FBI's adherence to its exclusive reliance on rapport-building techniques was Assistant Director Pasquale D'Amuro, who stressed in high-level meetings that force techniques, even though apparently approved by the White House Office of Legal Counsel, would produce false information, would make any testimony received from the detainee inadmissible in court, and would in the long run be the subject—he predicted—of a Congressional hearing.

[50] The *Review of the FBI's Involvement* acknowledges that the FBI reports understate what took place: agents had access only to military interrogation centers, not to the CIA black holes; FBI agents at Abu Ghraib never saw the inside of the building where the events that later became notorious took place, and the agents were never on the ground at night, when most abusive acts occurred. FBI rules required that the agent leave the room if any act incompatible with the FBI's own procedures began. Therefore agents were able to report only what they witnessed at the opening of a session. Only the classified version of the *Review of the FBI's Involvement* contains the full description of what FBI agents witnessed in the interrogations of "high value" detainees such as Abu Zubaydah.

[51] 28. U. S. Const. Sec 535.

[52] *Review of the FBI's Involvement.*

[53] Ibid. One agent in Afghanistan contacted headquarters to ask how much time had to elapse between the abusive non-FBI interrogation and his own in order for the information he received not to be contaminated by that other interrogation. The *Review of the FBI's Involvement* concludes that the FBI still has not answered this critically important question.

[54] Ibid.

[55] Ibid.

[56] Hugh Williamson, "Germany Seeks Arrest of 13 'CIA Agents,'" *Financial Times*, January 31, 2007.

[57] Tony Barber, "Americans to Stand Trial in Rendition Case," *Financial Times*, February 16, 2007. Judge Caterina Interlandi also charged the former head of the Italian intelligence service for the assistance he allegedly gave to the American agents.

[58] Tom Burgis, "Poland, Italy 'Colluded on CIA Detentions,'" *Financial Times*, November 28, 2006; and Andrew Bounds, "MEPs Condemn Rendition Flights," *Financial Times*, February 14, 2007.

[59] Sands, P. 2008. *Torture Team: Rumsfeld's Memo and the Betrayal of American Values*. Britain's handling of Spain's request for Pinochet's extradition is described at length in Sands's earlier book: Sands, P. 2005. *Lawless World*. New York: Penguin, 2005.

[60] U.S. Congress. House of Representatives. Kucinich, D. June 9, 2008. "Article 10." *Articles of Impeachment for President George W. Bush*. Washington, D.C.

[61] U.S. Department of Defense. "Operation Iraqi Freedom (OIF) U.S. Casualty Status Fatalities as of: August 18, 2008, 10 a.m. EDT." *DoD Casualty Reports*.

[62] *Review of the FBI's Involvement*. See also "Interrogation Log of Detainee 063, Day 28, December 20, 2002." in Sands, P. 2008 *Torture Team: Rumsfeld's Memo and the Betrayal of American Values*. Sands ends each chapter by including a passage from the

interrogation log of detainee al-Qahtani, a deeply effective way of alerting the reader to the concrete discrepancy between one's freedom to read and what happened to this prisoner over 54 consecutive days of torture. One inevitably feels, after one turns the page to start a new chapter and enters into the fascinating details of life in Washington D.C., that one has left the torture itself behind, only to be reminded at this new chapter's end that the torture continues. Though the time it takes to read the book is half a day, al-Qahtani was tortured for 54 days. Interrupting the reading act with the record of his torture acquaints the reader with the sense of unending time.

[63] Boed, R. 2000. "The Effect of a Domestic Amnesty on the Ability of Foreign States to Prosecute Alleged Perpetrators of Serious Human Rights Violations." *Cornell International Law Journal* 33(297).

[64] Grave breaches include "willful killing, torture, or inhuman treatment, including . . . willfully causing great suffering or serious injury to body or health, extensive destruction of property not justified by military necessity, willfully depriving a civilian of the rights of a fair and regular trial, and unlawful confinement of a civilian." Scharf, M. 1997. "Accountability for International Crime and Serious Violations of Fundamental Human Rights: the Letter of the Law: the Scope of the International Legal Obligation to Prosecute Human Rights Crimes." *Law & Contemporary Problems* 59 (4): 41–61.

[65] Ibid. Because the wording requires "submitting the case" to prosecution rather than requiring "prosecution," some analysts have seen the Convention as less than absolute; but Scharf compellingly argues that the "submit for prosecution" language is there to allow for the possibility that the person's innocence or

the lack of evidence then leads to a release from prosecution. On this point, see Scharf and Boed.

[66] Scharf, M. 1997. "Accountability for International Crime and Serious Violations of Fundamental Human Rights: the Letter of the Law: the Scope of the International Legal Obligation to Prosecute Human Rights Crimes."

[67] Boed, R. 2000. "The Effect of a Domestic Amnesty on the Ability of Foreign States to Prosecute Alleged Perpetrators of Serious Human Rights Violations."

BOSTON REVIEW BOOKS

Boston Review Books is an imprint of *Boston Review*, a bimonthly magazine of ideas. The book series, like the magazine, is animated by hope, committed to equality, and convinced that the imagination eludes political categories. Visit bostonreview.net for more information.